turtles
for home
and garden
by willy jocher

Distributed in the U.S.A. by T.F.H. Publications, Inc., 211 West Sylvania Avenue, P.O. Box 27, Neptune City, N.J. 07753; in England by T.F.H. (Gt. Britain) Ltd., 13 Nutley Lane, Reigate, Surrey; in Canada by Clarke, Irwin & Company, Clarwin House, 791 St. Clair Avenue West, Toronto 10, Ontario; in Southeast Asia by Y. W. Ong, 9 Lorong 36 Geylang, Singapore 14; in Australia and the south Pacific by Pet Imports Pty. Ltd., P.O. Box 149, Brookvale 2100, N.S.W., Australia.
Published by T.F.H. Publications, Inc. Ltd., The British Crown Colony of Hong Kong.

CONTENTS

FOREWORD

Turtles are not the most popular of pets, even though many of them are sold as pets each year, but to many people they are among the best pets available. They are inexpensive and comparatively easy to care for, and much can be learned about and from them.

Unfortunately, people who obtain pet turtles usually don't know much about how to keep them, and the turtles suffer because of their owners' lack of knowledge of their requirements. My intention in this book is to provide practical information and recommendations based on my own long experience with shelled reptiles. I hope that this book will help to secure long and pleasant lives for many pet turtles while making things easier for their owners.

CHAPTER ONE. INTRODUCTION TO THE TURTLES

The word 'pet' brings to mind cats, dogs, canaries, and other warm-blooded mammals and birds. These are all animals which can, to at least a minor degree, return a feeling of being appreciated, petted, or talked to. The cold-blooded fish, frogs, and lizards often kept are seldom referred to as pets. This is because they are just objects waiting to be fed every few hours or days and looked at occasionally. Turtles are the exception to this because some species seem to be capable of returning affection like a warm-blooded animal — or so their owners believe.

The turtles are a very old group of reptiles (reptiles include lizards, snakes, alligators, and dinosaurs as well as turtles) which have become very specialized for a slow, easy-going life. The armored shell, a dorsal carapace or back piece and a ventral plastron or belly piece, is formed from the ribs and other bones of the turtle's body. It cannot be shed like the carapace of a lobster or grasshopper. No living turtle has teeth, but all species have heavy plates on both jaws.

Turtles were once more common than they are today, and there were giant species on most continents. Even North America had several species with a carapace length of over three feet. Today's turtles are mostly small forms, few exceeding one foot in length. There are still a few giants, mainly among the sea turtles and the tortoises of remote islands, but even these are rapidly becoming extinct, thanks to man's greediness and ill-conceived concept of progress.

In a technical sense, all the shelled reptiles are properly called turtles. Even herpetologists, the scientists who study reptiles

7

The red-ear *(Pseudemys scripta elegans)* is a typical water turtle, easily recognized as such by the broadly webbed fore and hind feet. The skin is usually thin and soft, and the shell is light. Photo by A. Leutscher.

The diamondback is the only turtle which is rightly called "terrapin." *Malaclemys terrapin* was once highly valued for food and is still eaten today. Photo by R. J. Church.

The parrot-beaked tortoise *(Homopus areolatus)* of Africa exhibits the stout elephantine feet, thick skin, and heavy shell which usually distinguish the tortoises. Remember, though, that some land turtles look much like tortoises in shape. Photo by M. F. Roberts.

and amphibians (frogs, salamanders), however, commonly make a distinction between turtles, which live in or near the water, and tortoises, which live almost entirely on land. This distinction will be used throughout this book because care and feeding, as well as the type of pen required, will depend on whether you are keeping turtles or tortoises. Terrapin is an American Indian word applied to any edible water turtle. Since such a word is not needed in the pet field, no distinction will be made between turtles and terrapins; after all, who wants to eat his pet?

Tortoises are almost all from tropical or subtropical climates. Although many do inhabit deserts, there are numerous species which are found only in forests. All species of tortoises require warm temperatures, and most like to bask in the sun for a few hours each day. No tortoise, even a desert species, can take direct sunlight during the hottest part of the day for more than a few minutes; reptiles are as sensitive to over-heating as to cooling.

As a general rule tortoises are vegetarians, but a few will occasionally eat meat. Most require a water bath every day or two, and some even need to soak several hours a day; a few obtain most of their water from the food they eat.

Turtles usually have distinctly webbed hind feet and move slowly on land. Many species are carnivorous or insectivorous, but many other species are omnivores, eating both plants and meat or insects. Few species are strictly herbivorous; some side-necks and cooters are the examples which come to mind. All require easy access to water because of their thin, unprotected skin; many can swallow their food only under water.

The box turtles and a few other species are in some respects intermediate between the turtles and tortoises. Although they are closely related to the water turtles of the family Emydidae, they have thick, heavily scaled skin and strong legs with little or no webbing between the toes. Some species can even survive in desert or near-desert habitats, but most need frequent baths. Box turtles are famous for their durability, being able to adapt to many different types of conditions. Other species with similar adaptability are found in the genus *Geoemyda;* they are occasionally sold in pet shops.

Before buying a turtle or tortoise, decide which type of habitat will be easiest to maintain in your locality. Although extensive instructions are given on building outdoor quarters, I of course realize that such quarters will be beyond the means of most of the readers of this book, either for financial reasons or lack of space. Your pet will probably be kept indoors, where it can be more easily treated as a member of the family. Tortoises are easier to keep indoors than turtles, since they can be allowed the run of a well-heated apartment or put in an easily cleaned terrarium. Water turtles require filtration and well-built tanks. As a rule, tortoises show more interest in their surroundings than turtles, and they usually recognize their owner; many tortoises enjoy being petted. Water turtles often remain nervous, and some may be vicious; on the other hand, some are as intelligent

Although most turtles are omnivorous, a few are vegetarians. This yellow-spotted Amazon turtle *(Podocnemis unifilis)* is one such species. Photo by R. J. Church.

and responsive as tortoises. Turtles are also less expensive to purchase than most tortoises.

Whichever species you decide to keep, just remember that they are pets, not playthings. They must be fed, cleaned, and given attention. Turtles are not toys to be discarded after an afternoon of interest. A well treated turtle or tortoise might easily outlive any dog or cat, and some may even outlive you... so don't neglect them.

The common snapping turtle *(Chelydra serpentina)* is a vicious predator which will even eat small ducks. Photo by the American Museum of Natural History.

CHAPTER TWO. OUTDOOR TERRARIA

Tortoises are "children of the sun." To remain healthy and develop normally, they need a lot of sun and warmth. Their body temperature depends entirely on that of their environment, as opposed to birds and mammals, which when in health keep their body temperatures constant independent of the external temperature. When building an outdoor terrarium, it is this point which has to be borne in mind more than anything else. In practice this means that the outdoor terrarium must not be set up under a tree or too near a building, but of course not in a depression in the ground either, where the subsoil water could seep in or water accumulate from heavy showers. It is of particular importance to ensure good drainage of the terrarium.

THE PERMANENT TERRARIUM

The tortoise terrarium must not be too small. If the sides are three to four meters long, the terrarium can be both attractive and useful, and several specimens of various species can be kept in it. Species which grow to a large size can also be kept in it without our being afraid of not giving the animals enough room. Only weatherproof materials are suitable for use in construction: natural stones, cement, plastic sheeting, or wire-reinforced glass. Never use wood, plywood, or laminated wood. The enclosure should not look like a foreign body, but has to fit in well with the whole layout of the garden.

CONSTRUCTION

Start off by marking the outside wall with small posts. Carefully remove the grass, cutting it into fairly thick squares with a spade. The squares of grass are put flat on the ground side by side close to the building site, because we shall later use some of them again. In dry weather they have to be watered every day so that they stay green and the soil does not crumble away. Then excavate the whole area to a depth of twenty-five centimeters and dig a small trench with a depth of fifty centimeters along all four sides. This trench will later hold the foundation of the outside wall.

Pour some good concrete into the trench and then prepare a small form into which is poured the external wall, which is to be ten centimeters thick. Into the fresh concrete put 4 cm. thick poles to get the necessary hollow spaces for the corner and intermediate posts to be built and poured in later. The bottom surface is leveled and then covered by a four-centimeter deep layer of very coarse gravel or broken stone. On top of this put a seven-centimeter deep layer of slag concrete (if slag is not available, make a very thin concrete with coarse gravel). Although this whole surface is far from watertight, we still provide the whole area with a two percent slope toward the front.

Since we want to plant this small landscape as well, we must not forget to leave holes into which the plants will be put later. One method which has proved very suitable is to insert large flowerpots (with a diameter of thirty centimeters), the bottoms of which have been carefully knocked out before use. Bury the pot deeply enough so that its upper edge does not overlap the surface of the concrete.

ROCKWORK

When the cement has set we can start to build the rockwork. The bottom part of the group of rocks is made into a large cave which the tortoises will later like to use as their sleeping quarters, but which will also offer them shade when it is very hot. The cave is best made with bricks which have been dipped in cement. For the ceiling use plastic sheeting about twenty millimeters thick. Later cover all this with natural stones so that the bricks and sheeting can no longer be seen. The rest of the building is done with bricks which are later covered, or with natural stones. All stones or bricks are laid into cement from the back and afterwards form a single block which the animals cannot dislodge. When arranging this group of stones, there is one thing we must not forget: tortoises are very good climbers. A few projecting stone tiles will prevent the animals from climbing over.

Most tortoises, such as this forest hinge-back *(Kinixys homeana)*, require warm surroundings. Most (but not all) like to bask in the sun—but too much sunlight can kill any tortoise. Photo by G. Marcuse.

Our group of stones with a cave is suitable to house temperate climate land tortoises, but if we want to keep tropical species as well — for instance, *Geochelone elegans, G. radiata, G. pardalis, G. sulcata,* or *G. denticulata* — the stones have to be arranged to form a cavity with room for an electric heater. The simplest way to build such a hollow rock for tropical land tortoises is to use plaster fabric which can be obtained at any building material shop. This fabric is very pliable and can be folded and bent to the desired shape. It is then fixed to the slag concrete with cement. With the help of a trowel, the shaped fabric is given three coats of cement (a thick pulp, mixture one to three), each at an interval of one day. After the third coating no more holes should be visible. On the following day apply pure cement pulp with a brush to get an even surface. To make the construction look more natural, the cement can be colored with water paint. To heat the cave, hang up two small 50 W infrared lamps inside. A small cover closes up the heating channel at the top; of course, the cover has to be fitted in such a way that no rain water can get in.

WATER BASIN

Into the front left corner put a small cement water basin. If its diameter is 25 centimeters and its depth 7 centimeters, it is large enough for our purposes. A plastic pipe with a diameter of 25 millimeters is built in to serve as drain. The drain is sealed with a rubber stopper from the outside, because valves keep getting blocked when the water basin is cleaned. A sieve supposed to protect the drain pipe from leaves, gravel, or food remainders has proved unsuitable, since the tortoises are forever pressing against and removing it.

All around the small basin, lay tiles of natural stone. They must not be rough; the shells of the tortoises might get damaged. When they have all been fitted, lay them into a cement pulp, which should not be too thick (mixture one to one), and knock them down with the handle of the hammer so that they are exactly level with the upper edge of the water basin. The cement pulp squeezed out at the joints is wiped off immediately. Two days later, when the cement has set, we do the pointing. The grass squares are now laid close to the stone tiles, keeping the joints between the sods as narrow as possible. Finally, fill in the cracks with good compost soil.

Into the cavity under the group of rocks put a five-centimeter deep layer of coarse sand. Here the tortoises will like to dig holes in which to hide. The four corner posts are made from angle iron with a thickness of forty millimeters; for the intermediate posts use forty-millimeter thick T-iron. After the necessary holes have been bored, the posts are put into the spaces provided for them and secured with cement (mixture one to one). The two side walls and the back wall are made from tiles which are sixty centimeters high and twenty millimeters thick. For the long front wall use wire reinforced or plate glass, ten to twelve millimeters thick. The tiles are fastened on with screws, but the glass panes lie in a rubber channel and are secured with angle iron twenty millimeters thick. If we intend to house large tortoises in the terrarium, the lower edge of the pane should be protected by a wooden board against knocks. The tiles can be painted dark or olive green with a concrete paint. This makes the whole construction more pleasing to the eye. To make the outer walls from cement or bricks is, of course, also possible, but such constructions look heavy and awkward. Before inserting the tiles and the glass, all iron parts are given a coat of non-toxic waterproofing compound to make sure they do not rust.

To keep this enclosure clean is no problem. The food is always put down on the stone tiles, from which the leftovers are easy to remove. The tiles and water basin are scrubbed daily with a little water and a brush, preventing unpleasant smells and the gathering of flies.

DECORATIONS

Perennial plants are put in during the autumn. Others, which would not survive the winter outdoors, are planted in spring.

The pots are secured with small stones so that the tortoises cannot knock them over, and empty spaces are filled in with soil. To prevent the tortoises from mowing down the bushes, knock a strong post into the pot (the bottom of which has already been removed) before planting and saw it off thirty centimeters above the bottom. We then tie the plant to this post.

If you are able to take fairly large non-perennial plants indoors for the winter, you can turn the outdoor terrarium into a beautiful piece of miniature scenery. There are many different plants you

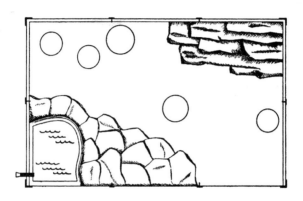

Diagram (above) of possible arrangement of the outdoor terrarium. The water bowl and caves or rockpiles in the corners are necessary, but the potted plants (circles) can be changed as desired. Below is one method of placing rock slabs to form a cave of the desired size

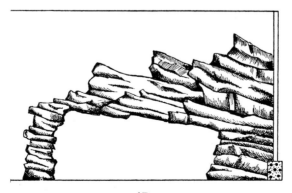

could use for this, but try to match the scenery to the natural habitat of your tortoises.

If they have been kept cool during the winter, non-perennial plants can be transferred to the outdoor terrarium by early spring. Be sure that the enclosure is covered with a plastic sheet if there is still a chance of frosts.

TEMPORARY TERRARIA

WIRE ENCLOSURE

Land tortoises can, of course, also be kept in simpler and less expensive open air enclosures.

With only ten meters of fine mesh wire and six wooden posts, we can put up a small wire run of two by three meters. The wire netting is then simply buried in the ground for a depth of ten centimeters. A simple enclosure like this can be made to look very pleasant, too. A tree trunk with plenty of branches, a few fairly large stones overgrown with moss, and two or three medium-sized bushes, for example, can create an attractive miniature landscape where the animals feel happy. It is important that we choose a sunny site; the bushes provide sufficient shade, but even the simplest enclosure has to have a sheltered sleeping place, perhaps under a tree trunk. As a water bowl, a bird bath of natural stone is used.

BOX ENCLOSURE

Less attractive but very easy to build is an open-air enclosure made like a sandbox for children. The material for this can be planks, cement, or plastic sheeting. The front plank, facing south, should be slanting to give shade to the animals even in the full glare of the sun. Two horizontal planks on the narrow sides, one ten centimeters broad, the other thirty centimeters, serve as covering for the sleeping place. At the same time they prevent the tortoises, which have a special preference for climbing up in the corners, from escaping. The whole box is securely anchored in the ground with four wooden or iron posts so that the tortoises cannot slip through at the bottom either. On one third of the surface remove the grass and replace it with a five-centimeter deep layer of medium coarse gravel. Into the gravel layer set a drinking bowl and a stone tile, which should not be too small, to serve as a feeding place. When it is cold or raining, or overnight, we can cover the whole pen with hot-bed windows. As the marketable size of a hot-bed window is 100 by 150 centimeters, calculate the dimensions of the open-air enclosure accordingly.

Since the front plank slants in this very simple type of enclosure, we get a gradient of about four centimeters, which is perfectly adequate to ensure that the rainwater runs off quickly. When the sun is shining the box must never be completely covered, or the heat would build up and the animals would come to harm. It would also be a mistake to cover the pen immediately whenever there is a small rain shower. A short spell of warm rain is good for our tortoises; it makes them grow lively, especially if it has been preceded by a fairly long period of dry weather.

If you want to have a still cheaper covering for the open-air enclosure, you can make frames of suitable size with the help of roof laths and cover them with plastic sheeting. But these light frames have to be weighted or provided with small hooks, otherwise the wind might blow them away.

CHAPTER THREE.   INDOOR TERRARIA

Other than their apartment, many people who live in the city do not have the smallest spot of land available to them, and often the lease prohibits the keeping of dogs and cats.   For those who still wish to keep a pet, the land tortoise is an ideal sub-tenant: it is not noisy, does not bite, makes little mess, and only requires a small warm spot.   On the cold kitchen floor, however, it is not happy.   It feels much more comfortable on a warm wooden floor.

LET IT RUN LOOSE!

The moment a sunbeam comes through the open window and shines on the floor boards, our tortoise is there; then there is no titbit that could lure it away from the warming sunshine.   In summer a balcony or a large terrace is ideal, for here the tortoise can bask in the sun and sunbathe all summer long.   But we have to make sure it cannot fall off, for a fall is painful and the shell is by no means as robust as is often thought.   A plank thirty centimeters in width, fastened to the railing with staples, protects the animal from falling off.

If the sun burns down for several hours, however, the concrete floor of the balcony grows so hot that even tortoise feet begin to feel uncomfortable.   Then the animal needs a shaded spot.   A little shade can be provided quite easily: a kitchen stool or a chair gives sufficient shade.   More suitable would be a 'napping box.'   From a small but not too shallow box, remove one narrow side and knock away any nails that may be sticking out.   The tortoise will appreciate this shelter and there, in the semi-darkness, have its afternoon nap.

That we need a water bowl goes without saying. It should have a diameter of ten to fifteen centimeters and be about four centimeters deep. To make sure it does not get knocked over all the time, glue it onto a thin plank or a sheet of thick cardboard.

If the family goes for a weekend drive into the country, the tortoise can come along. Let it roam freely in a meadow where it can look for delicious herbs and tender grasses it never gets at home. Of course we have to watch that it does not get lost in knee-high grass and vanish from sight. For if the whole family goes off in search of it, often for hours, the pleasure is great when at long last the animal has been found again, but the farmer whose beautiful grass has been brutally trampled will not be very pleased. That must never happen again. So the next time put a rubber band, two to three centimeters broad, around the shell of our tortoise and tie a brightly colored balloon to it. Now we do not have to look for it and can save ourselves a lot of trouble and worry.

A warm sleeping place will also have to be provided if the tortoise is left to move about freely in the apartment during the day. The species which do not hibernate especially need a sleeping place. Particularly in spring or in autumn, when the heating is no longer or not yet on, the floor in the flat is far too cold for the tortoise. Then we should hang up a small infrared lamp during the day, sixty centimeters above the floor, preferably near the window. It is here, in this warm spot, that we should feed the tortoise, too. At night the tortoises like to hide away in some corner or under a piece of furniture, and if it is a cool night they very easily catch severe colds.

Tortoises, particularly the tropical species, should be kept in a heated sleeping box over night.

In the tropical native countries of the tortoises, the temperature also drops sharply at night, but during the day the sandy, stony ground has absorbed so much heat that even by night it does not grow too cold. With a weak floor heater we can imitate these conditions. At night the sleeping box is, therefore, not heated from the top with a ray lamp, but from the bottom with a heating cable. The dimensions of the sleeping box depend on the number of animals we want to keep in it and whether they are species which grow to a large size. 80 by 40 by 40 centimeters, for instance, would be suitable. The bottom of the box has to be well insulated to prevent heat loss. First put a three-centimeters-deep layer of insulating wool into the box; this is covered with ten-millimeter thick plastic sheeting. Onto the walls, over the sheeting, glue four-centimeter broad strips of plastic which carry a second piece of sheeting to form a second bottom. Into the four-centimeter high space between the two bottom plates, put a 13 W heating cable. Finally the box is furnished with a four-centimeter layer of gravel, which should not be too fine. If the box is in a cool room, we can provide it with a cover but must not forget to make enough air holes in the two side walls.

Somewhat delicate species and all others that require plenty of warmth — *Geochelone radiata, G. elegans,* and the young of *Geochelone pardalis* and *G. sulcata,* for instance — should be kept in a heated indoor terrarium during the winter, after having spent the summer in an outdoor terrarium that was also heated. As a heater use a ground heating cable which is switched on overnight. During the day an infrared lamp keeps the temperature at about 25° C.

THE TERRARIUM

There is no reason why a tortoise terrarium should look barren. Along the back wall we can make a small wall from beautiful stones and turn the top part into a plant bowl. The wall is held together with cement and allowed to lean forward a little so that the animals cannot climb over it. A bath container is not put in because it takes up too much room and makes the terrarium too wet. The tortoises can be taken out of the terrarium to be given their bath. But a small drinking bowl must be provided, as well as a stone tile for food. This tile is simply embedded in the gravel so that we can take it out easily to wash it. The gravel, too, is taken out at regular intervals and washed thorough-

A terrarium need not be large or fancy to satisfy a tortoise's basic needs, but it must be clean and warm and provide exercise room for the tortoise. Photos by R. J. Church.

ly. Afterwards rinse it with boiling water. In this way we control parasites and prevent unpleasant smells. Only a meticulously clean terrarium will ensure that our pets remain healthy for many years.

CHAPTER FOUR.   CARE AND FEEDING

EXTERNAL PARASITES

Newly acquired tortoises must never be put into a terrarium immediately, as the whole enclosure might all to easily become infested with ectoparasites.   Before doing anything else, we must give the new pet a thorough examination.   For this put the animal on a table which is covered with white paper or cloth.

Ticks are the most frequent ectoparasites of tortoises.   These tormentors usually sit in the skin folds at the base of the tail, but are found around the neck, too, and even at the corners of the eye and the mouth.   The ticks bury themselves in the flesh, and it would be a mistake to try to pull them out with tweezers, since their mouthparts would stay behind in the skin and severe inflammations could result.   It is really quite simple to remove ticks. Dab the attached tick with olive oil; the oil blocks the respiratory organs of the parasite, which then dies of asphyxia and falls off. Young ticks, which are still very small, are easily overlooked. To get rid of them, too, treatment with cod liver ointment has proved very successful.   Warm some ointment in a small tin lid and then apply the ointment, which is now liquid, to all soft parts of the animal, including the edges of the eyes and the corners of the mouth.   A brush is very useful for this purpose.   After one hour the ointment is wiped off with a soft cloth.

If, instead of ticks, we discover small mites, the cod liver ointment is equally helpful.   This ointment makes the skin smooth and supple and any sores caused by ticks or mites will quickly heal.

WORMS

Afterward the tortoise is washed with warm water (30 to 35° C). For this use a small, soft, hand brush, particularly for the shell and the legs; for the soft parts and the head it is better to use a soft cloth. A warm bath stimulates peristaltic movement; usually the tortoise will then pass feces, which can be examined for intestinal worms. If worms are present, it is best to see a veterinarian because treatment with vermicides is not altogether without danger for the animal. It is important, above all, before any treatment is given for worms, to establish what kind of intestinal worms are present so that the correct agent and dosage can be applied.

Some types of worms can be controlled with the aid of a carrot diet given for several days. The carrots are grated and given to the tortoises without anything being added to them. During this five-day course of treatment, no other food must be offered and the feces are examined for worms every day. If this mild treatment is unsuccessful, we have to go to the veterinarian after all. Almost all land tortoises like carrots. If they do not take the food on the first day, we simply let them fast for two to three days until they do eat it.

After the bath, dry the shell and rub it very thinly with mineral oil. The animals must be given a bath in tepid water every week; this is absolutely essential for their health and well-being. If it is cool outside, they must not be put into the outdoor terrarium immediately after the bath. They would inevitably catch a cold.

FOOD

VEGETABLES

With few exceptions, land tortoises are vegetarians. Hence it is not difficult to feed them and to get food for them. Brightly colored fruits or flowers, particularly red ones, are often preferred.   Apples, pears, plums, tomatoes, and beets are given finely diced.   Overripe bananas, on the other hand, can be given whole (without the skin).   For large tortoises such as *Geochelone sulcata* and *G. pardalis,* cut up the banana together with the skin. Small berries such as strawberries, raspberries, blackberries, grapes, ripe elderberries, and cherries, peaches, apricots, sweet melons, oranges, mandarins, and even lemons sprinkled with sugar can be offered.   It is important that tortoises get plenty of variety, for it can happen that our tortoises stubbornly refuse a certain food for weeks and then suddenly, without any apparent reason, greedily take it again.

All tortoises like lettuce.   Parsley, chives, young beans, young peas, and the fresh leaves of peas are eaten with relish. All hard vegetables, such as cauliflower, kale, and white cabbage, have to be cut into small pieces.   Carrots and beets have to be scraped or peeled.   In spring, pick various types of flowers; especially enjoyed are blossoms of false acacia and coltsfoot.   In summer provide dandelion flowers and red clover.

Some animals will also take rice pudding, oatmeal cooked in milk, and white bread steeped in milk.   Just for a change offer raw minced meat as well from time to time, mixed with rice and shaped into small balls.

ANIMAL FOODS

Some tortoises are gourmets and have a special liking for slugs, earthworms, and fairly large insects.   I kept an adult *Geochelone radiata* which had to share its four square-meter terrarium with a young monitor lizard.   Every day for several weeks, it devoured rather large quantities of scalded beetles which were really meant for the monitor.   A 25-centimeter long *Geochelone sulcata* was kept in the company of two large teiid lizards. The teiids were given raw eggs and raw horsemeat cut into finger-long strips.   No sooner had this food been put into the terrarium than the tortoise hurried towards it and even pushed the lizards aside to be the first to have a meal — and yet there was a bowl waiting for it with fresh lettuce, pears, and tomatoes!

Finally I would like to draw your attention to an excellent food of high nutritional value: germinated wheat. This is greedily eaten by all tortoises, and there is no better food for the rearing of baby tortoises, particularly during the winter months.

Food supplements should be given to all turtles and tortoises regularly. The many preparations on the market are all designed to provide the vitamins and minerals your pet may not get from his regular food. Photo courtesy of Wardley Pet Products.

SUPPLEMENTS

People often forget that tortoises need calcium. They require a lot of calcium for the development of the shell, especially young animals which are still growing. Finely ground bonemeal should be mixed into the food each day. A pinch is sufficient. Bonemeal can usually be purchased at pet shops, and nurseries always have it in stock. Several commercial turtle vitamin preparations are available and should also be mixed with the food occasionally.

Most of these are based on fish oil and are messy to handle and feed. Tablets are also available. These should be ground and mixed with the food. Calcium and vitamin D can only be properly utilized by the body if the animals are subjected to as much direct sunlight as possible. During the cold months when there is little sun, we make do with an ultraviolet lamp. Two to three irradiations, of five minutes each, per week are sufficient. The most favorable distance between the lamp and the ground lies about eighty centimeters.

FEEDING TIME

When shall we feed? With any pet it is extremely important to stick to certain feeding times. Tortoises very quickly get to the fact that they receive food, say, every day at 11 o'clock in the morning. Their whole day and life rhythm will become adjusted to this. Land tortoises should be fed late in the forenoon, for it is at this time that they are most active. Animals which have been living in captivity for some time and are well nourished are only given as much food as they are able to eat within two hours. It is not good to leave food lying around in the terrarium all day long. It wilts and dries up and the valuable vitamins are very quickly destroyed, particularly when the food is lying in the sun. One to two fasting days per week have proved advantageous; they prevent the fatty degeneration of vital organs.

Young animals which are still growing are offered nourishing and varied food every day, without a fasting day inbetween, preferably two or three times daily. With newly acquired tortoises we must experiment with all sorts of foods to find out what they like. When tortoises are kept singly, several days will often elapse before they take food for the first time. If several are kept together, they will usually start sooner; tortoises, too, are jealous of each other.

If we already have a fairly large stock of acclimated animals in our terrarium and wish to add a new animal, perhaps even a young

In order to grow up healthy and well-formed, the baby tortoise must be fed regularly on a varied diet of the fruits and vegetables it enjoys most. Sunlight and vitamin supplements will help it endure the occasional diseases it is likely to encounter. Photo by I. Ashmore.

one, the new arrival should be given extra food, at least during the first few weeks. The hardships of importation have usually weakened the animal. Put the animal into a small box where it is undisturbed and able to get enough to eat. Once the tortoise gets its strength back, it will be able to hold its own among the old ones and refuse to be chased away from the food dish.

CHAPTER FIVE. COMMON TORTOISES

HERMANN'S TORTOISE

Hermann's tortoise and the Mediterraneñ spur-thighed tortoise are probably the tortoises most commonly kept in Europe. *Testudo hermanni* lives in Dalmatia, Albania, Greece, Syria, Rumania, Bulgaria, southern Hungary, and southern Italy. Hermann's tortoise is commonly offered in European pet shops in all sizes and is especially common in spring.

The carapace of Hermann's tortoise is moderately domed, broadens towards the back and is steeper there than at the front. Every shield of the carapace is black in the center and has a black margin. The background color is yellow to brown. Legs, head, and neck are greenish yellow in color. The supracaudal shield is almost always divided into two. The females grow slightly larger than the males, reaching a length of 25 to 30 centimeters; they can be distinguished from the males by the thicker but shorter tails. In both sexes there is a claw-like horny terminal on the tail. The plastron of the female looks flat, that of the male is slightly concave; this sexual difference also applies to most other turtles as well.

The western subspecies of Hermann's tortoise, *Testudo hermanni robertmertensi,* is found in southwestern Europe: southern France, eastern Spain, the Balearic Islands, Sardinia, and Corsica. This beautiful tortoise is seldom seen in the pet shops. It differs from *Testudo hermanni hermanni* by its more highly domed carapace, which is more intensively colored as well. Its most striking characteristic is a bright yellow spot under the eye.

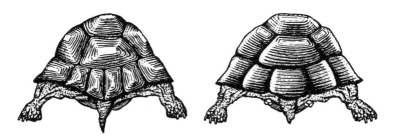

Although superficially very much alike, Hermann's tortoise *(Testudo hermanni)* and the Mediterranean spur-thighed tortoise *(Testudo graeca)* are easily distinguished. *T. hermanni* (left) has the supracaudal shield divided into two shields and lacks a pair of warts on each side of the root of the tail. *T. graeca* (right) has an undivided supracaudal and a pair of warts on each side of the tail root.

Testudo hermanni is probably the most commonly kept European tortoise. Only *T. hermanni* and its close relatives in the Middle East and Mediterranean area now belong to the genus *Testudo*, the other species having been transferred to *Geochelone.* Photo by R. J. Church.

Testudo horsfieldi is found as far west as India and just reaches European Russia. It has thigh warts like *T. graeca*, but has only four claws on the front feet. Photo by G. Marcuse.

Two of the several subspecies of *Testudo graeca* are shown here. The large specimen is *T. g. zarudnyi*, the small one *T. g. graeca*. Photo by P. C. H. Pritchard.

Geochelone pardalis, the leopard tortoise of Africa, is a large, variable species highly valued by collectors. Photo by Dr. Herbert R. Axelrod.

MEDITERRANEAN SPUR-THIGHED TORTOISE

At first glance, the inexperienced will fail to notice much difference between Hermann's tortoise and the Mediterranean spur-thighed tortoise, *Testudo graeca*.

The supracaudal shield is never divided and the tail shows no horny terminal. The surest marks of identification are two large, wart-like horny tubercles on the back of the thigh, on the right and left of the tail root. Size and sex differences are the same as in Hermann's tortoise. The color of the carapace varies greatly. In some animals the basic overall color is olive-green and there are hardly any black markings. Others again possess beautiful markings on a yellow-brown background.

The distribution of the Mediterranean spur-thighed tortoise ranges from southern Europe via North Africa to Asia Minor and Persia. There are four subspecies. None occur in Greece.

Hatchlings of *Testudo marginata* and all other tortoises are sensitive to temperature changes. The mortality rate from pneumonia is often high. Photo by O. Stemmler.

The thin, inflatable shell of the African pancake tortoise *(Mala-cochersus tornieri)* enables it to hide in cracks between rocks. It then swallows air, inflating the shell and wedging it into place. This is certainly one of the most unusual of the tortoises. Photo by G. Marcuse.

MARGINED TORTOISE

The margined tortoise, *Testudo marginata,* lives in Greece, predominantly in the southern provinces. It is the largest and most beautiful of the three European species, but unfortunately is seldom imported. The lateral marginal shields of the carapace fall away fairly vertically, but the posterior marginals, on the other hand, are very broad and project widely, rather like a fireman's helmet. In coloration the young animals resemble Hermann's tortoise, but the older animals are usually dark, almost black.

Adults of South American forest tortoises are fairly easy to distinguish. *Geochelone carbonaria* usually has a smooth front margin to the carapace. The sides are often strongly indented ("dumbbell"), and the leg color is normally red. *Geochelone denticulata* often retains the toothed front carapace margin even as an adult; it has parallel sides. The leg color is normally yellow. In both pictures, *Geochelone carbonaria* is to the left, *G. denticulata* to the right. Photos by P. C. H. Pritchard.

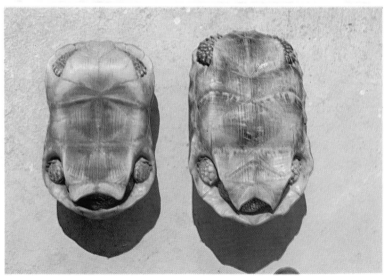

The Florida subspecies of the eastern box turtle *(Terrapene carolina bauri)* resembles the western box turtle, but the plastron is light with dark streaks. Photo by Dr. Herbert R. Axelrod.

The "starred" pattern found on the Indian star tortoise *(Geochelone elegans)* is also shared with several other African and Asian species. Photo by P. C. H. Pritchard.

SPURRED TORTOISE

This native of Africa attains a size of just under a meter. It lives in desert areas of Abyssinia and the southern Sudan west to Senegal. Its flat carapace is of a uniform light yellow to light brown, more rarely of a reddish brown color. The lateral marginal shields are almost vertical. The name spurred tortoise refers to two large spurs the animal carries on its thigh, a characteristic one cannot fail to notice.

Geochelone sulcata is a very lively tortoise which can be kept in the best of health for many years if it is looked after properly. It is commonly offered for sale, but unfortunately these are almost always nothing but medium to large animals like the ones we see in zoos. Young animals of this species are very long-lived in the terrarium and give their keeper much pleasure, not least because of their unusual liveliness.

The African spurred tortoise *(Geochelone sulcata)* is the largest tortoise in Africa. Photo by P. C. H. Pritchard.

The radiated tortoise *(Geochelone radiata)* of Madagascar is one of the most beautiful and sought-after-tortoises, but it unfortunately is rare. Photo by P. C. H. Pritchard.

LEOPARD TORTOISE

This African species is widely distributed, ranging from the upper Nile via Abyssinia to the Cape and in the west as far as Angola. The carapace of the leopard tortoise, *Geochelone pardalis,* is very highly domed and reaches a length of fifty centimeters. The animal owes the name leopard tortoise to its beautiful spotted back with an ochre-colored ground that is virtually seething with black spots and lines. The leopard tortoise also has a marked wart-like horny tubercle on the thigh.

It is very hardy in captivity and learns relatively quickly where to find its food, but remains somewhat timid and shy even after years. Young animals are much more colorful than adults and are excellently suited for the desert terrarium. Unfortunately this tortoise is rarely offered on the market and is quite expensive.

Eastern painted turtle *(Chrysemys picta picta)*. Notice the broad light bands on the carapace. Photo by Dr. Herbert R. Axelrod.

Reeves' turtle *(Chinemys reevesi)* is perhaps the most commonly kept Asian water turtle. Photo by Dr. Herbert R. Axelrod.

The southern painted turtle *(Chrysemys picta dorsalis)*. Photo by H. Peter.

The Indian roofed turtle *(Kachuga tecta)*. Photo by P. C. H. Pritchard.

Geochelone elegans is unusual in that it requires very little water. Moist food and an occasional warm bath in shallow water is sufficient. Photo by G. Marcuse.

INDIAN STARRED TORTOISE

The carapace of the Indian starred tortoise, *Geochelone elegans*, shows the same type of star-like markings as do those of several other tortoises. It lives in India and Ceylon, predominantly in dry areas where there are plants, and there it spends the hottest hours of the day under bushes and grass. It rarely drinks, so needs no water dish; it should be bathed every few weeks.

The elongated carapace is domed in the center. Each of the individual shields is raised to form a hump. The basic color of the carapace is brown, and the center of each shield is yellow or orange. Star-like stripes of yellow radiate from the center and unite with those of the neighboring shields.

The animal is somewhat delicate in captivity. But if we look after it well we can still keep it alive for many years and again and again its beautiful markings will fill us with renewed delight.

YELLOW-LEGGED TORTOISE

Of the three South American tortoises, only two commonly enter the terrarium trade. *Geochelone denticulata* and *Geochelone carbonaria* are commonly known as forest tortoises. *G. denticulata* is a large tortoise (usually 12 inches long, very rarely to 27 inches) with a brown carapace having a yellow spot in the center of each scute. The scales of the head and legs are usually bright orange or yellowish in color. Young specimens have the front edge of the carapace toothed, the roughness being lost with growth.

Like all tortoises, the yellow-legged is basically herbivorous, although it will accept some meat. Some even seem to enjoy canned dog foods. Feed it plenty of fruit and green vegetables. Since it is a tortoise of the deep forests, it does not commonly bask in the sun. Keep the temperature and humidity high.

The red-legged tortoise *(Geochelone carbonaria)* is one of the few South American turtles or tortoises commonly available to collectors. Photo by R. J. Church.

The most popular turtle: *Pseudemys scripta elegans*, the red-ear.
Photos by Dr. Herbert R. Axelrod.

The Colombian cooter *(Pseudemys scripta callirostris)* is easily recognized by a red ear mark and large yellow dots under the chin. Photo by Dr. Herbert R. Axelrod.

There are so many similar subspecies of the Florida cooter *(Pseudemys floridana)* that it is almost impossible to identify single specimens. Notice the distinctive carapace markings. Photo by Dr. Herbert R. Axelrod.

RED-LEGGED TORTOISE

This South American forest tortoise is very similar to the yellow-legged in both color and behavior. The carapace is black instead of brown, and the head and legs are usually marked with red instead of yellow. The anterior edge of the carapace is smooth in young tortoises, not toothed as in *G. denticulata*. Adult red-legged tortoises often develop a characteristic "dumbell" shape which is not seen in the yellow-legged. This tortoise often reaches 10 inches in length, but the largest known specimen is less than 18 inches long.

Both the yellow-legged and the red-legged tortoises are found over a large area of South America, from Colombia through the Guianas and south to Bolivia and central Brazil. The red-legged is also found in Panama (rare) and south to Paraguay and southern Brazil. It is also more likely to be found in open forests and savannas than is the yellow-legged.

The eastern box turtle *(Terrapene carolina carolina)* in its most familiar color pattern. The strongly hooked upper jaw is due to improper feeding. Photo by Dr. Herbert R. Axelrod.

The Florida box turtle *(Terrapene carolina bauri)*. Photo by Dr. Herbert R. Axelrod.

AMERICAN BOX TURTLES

The eastern box turtle, *Terrapene carolina,* is probably kept by more people than any other land turtle. Although seldom offered for sale by dealers, it is usually easily collected locally or obtained from aquaintances in the natural range of the species. There are many subspecies of this turtle, but all are basically similar in behavior, even when they differ greatly in color pattern.

The single hinge in the middle of the plastron readily identifies the box turtles. Although belonging to the same family (Emydidae) as most of the water turtles, these turtles lack well-developed webs between the toes and are more at home on land than in the water. The terrarium for box turtles should be mostly land with about one-fourth or so devoted to a water pan. Provide a good variety of fruits and vegetables, but also a large selection of insects, earthworms, slugs, and other assorted tidbits. Fresh drinking water should always be available.

The Florida red-bellied turtle *(Pseudemy nelsoni)* and its relatives belong to the *Rubriventris* species group of the genus. The red bars on the carapace are distinctive. Photo by P. C. H. Pritchard.

The several subspecies of the diamondback terrapin vary greatly in coloration and sculpturing of the shell. Photo by Dr. Herbert R. Axelrod.

Graptemys flavomarginatus is a rare map turtle from southern Mississippi and Alabama. Notice the great size difference between the female (left) and the male (right), both adults. Photo by P. C. H. Pritchard at the Bronx Zoo.

The color pattern of the head is very important in identifying map turtles. Without seeing the pattern behind the eye, it is not really possible to identify this young map. Photo by Dr. Herbert R. Axelrod.

Most of the American box turtles are dark brown with some type of yellow pattern on the carapace. In many individuals some scales on the head and legs may be bright red or at least orange. The eastern box turtle, *T. c. carolina,* is a very widely distributed turtle, ranging from northern Florida and Tennessee north to Michigan and New Hampshire. Three other subspecies, *T. c. bauri* (Florida), *T. c. major* (along the coast from Georgia to Louisiana), and *T. c. triunguis* (Georgia to Missouri and Texas, south), occur in the southern United States.

In the Great Plains states and the Southwest, *Terrapene carolina* is replaced by the very similar *Terrapene ornata.* This box turtle differs from the eastern mainly in that the yellow of the carapace is in the form of radiating lines and the plastron is mostly dark, with yellow lines. Its habits are similar to those of the eastern, but it is much less aquatic. It also feeds more on insects,

The box turtles are easily recognized by the combination of stout feet with little or no webbing and a single hinge on the plastron. Photo by G. Marcuse.

Young box turtles look quite different from the adult. The carapace is heavily sculptured, relatively low, and has a central row of nodules. The hinge is not visible until the turtle is about two inches long. Photo by R. J. Church.

and some specimens are especially fond of grasshoppers and raw meat.

Both box turtles have gained a reputation for longevity, and they probably deserve it. There are many individuals which are known to have been in captivity over 50 years, and a very old age of over 100 is suspected for a few specimens. Box turtles make good and, for turtles, intelligent pets. They are low in cost, easy to keep, and attractive in their behavior and colors.

The species of *Cuora* are often called Asian box turtles because they have become adapted to a more terrestrial existence than most other water turtles in their range. *Cuora trifasciata* (above), the three-lined box turtle, differs from the Malayan box turtle *(Cuora amboinensis*, below) in having a keeled shell and being more aquatic. Photos by P. C. H. Pritchard.

The stinkpot *(Sternotherus odoratus)* is one of the most common turtles in eastern North America. Its small size and durability make it a good species for the beginner, but recently caught specimens have a bad temper. Photo by Dr. Herbert R. Axelrod.

The many species of mud turtles *(Kinosternon)* are all suitable for the beginning turtle keeper, although they are not very colorful. The small plastron with two hinges is clearly shown in this photograph. Photo by P. C. H. Pritchard.

CHAPTER SIX. LIVING QUARTERS FOR AQUATIC TURTLES

The true element of aquatic turtles is stagnant or slowly flowing waters to which they retreat immediately if there is danger. Most aquatic turtles are excellent swimmers and divers, but on land, too, they are considerably quicker than terrestrial tortoises. Nor are they as good-natured as land tortoises; when we pick them up with our hands they try to resist us by scratching, kicking, and biting. With very few exceptions, aquatic turtles are predators. Everything that moves is snatched with their sharp jaws and, unless it is too big, swallowed whole while the head is thrust forward by jerks. If the prey is too large, the animals tear it to pieces with their sharp claws. Aquatic turtles which have been kept in captivity for some time, however, grow very tame, quickly get to know their keeper, and take food out of the hand.

Depending on their way of life, we can distinguish between two groups, diurnal and nocturnal animals. For the hobbyist the diurnal animals are, of course, the most interesting ones. They are the "children of the sun" that follow every sunbeam, and with their liveliness give their keeper much pleasure. The nocturnal animals only become properly active toward the evening, at dusk, and only then leave their daytime hiding place to go in search of food. Rarely they scramble out of the water to sunbathe. This is also true of the soft-shelled turtles, which bury themselves in the bottom layer with only the head sticking out to look for food.

THE OUTDOOR POOL

REQUIREMENTS

Of the greatest importance with regard to our outdoor pond is the site we choose for it. Throughout the year it has to remain unshaded, which means it must not be set up under large trees or right next to a building. It is also advantageous, almost a necessity, to be able to connect the basin with an existing drainage system. Aquatic turtles require a lot of food and consequently eject a great deal of fecal matter, which soon leads to fouling of the water. Fouling, however, must not be allowed to happen. If the animals are left in severely contaminated water for too long their health will be adversely affected. At best, the result would be badly healing eye damage. But we would not take pleasure in our turtles for very long either if it were not possible for us to clean the enclosure easily and within the shortest time. Once the problems of water supply, inflow of new water, and drainage of old water have been solved, the rest of the set-up is purely a matter of taste and does not affect the health of the animals as long as it satisfies their requirements in some measure.

BUILDING THE POND

When determing the external dimensions of the pool, particularly those of the water basin, we must bear in mind that the water stays clean for considerably longer in a large tank with a small stock than it does where conditions are the reverse. For pond turtles, the enclosure can never be large enough. Over and above that, a spacious pond can be designed to look more attractive and more natural and causes less work. For tropical species, on the other hand, the pond should not be more than two meters broad so that we can comfortably cover it with a plastic sheet at night. The length of the sheet is immaterial, but it can be rolled up more easily if strips of wood are nailed to the ends of the sheets.

The mata-mata *(Chelys fimbriata)* is probably the best known yet most bizarre side-neck. Although it is very sluggish, its large size still demands a large tank. Photo by H. Schultz.

The Indian soft-shell *(Lissemys punctata)* is very high-domed for a member of this group of turtles. The color pattern is unusually attractive. Photo by Dr. Herbert R. Axelrod.

Adults of the Florida soft-shell *(Trionyx ferox)* lose their blotched juvenile pattern and become almost uniformly dark. This large turtle can be very vicious. Photo by P. C. H. Pritchard.

A large alligator snapping turtle *(Macrochelys temmincki)* can have a head two feet in circumference, and a temper to match. The heavy sculpturing of the carapace distinguishes it from the common snapper. Photo by P. C. H. Pritchard.

For a drain pipe use a PVC pipe, 70 millimeters in diameter, one end of which is built into the concrete at the deepest part of the water basin. Before doing this, insert a brass connection to hold the end of the pipe. The drain pipe has to have a gradient of at least five percent, and there must be no deflections or pockets which would lead to frequent blocking later on.

When we excavate the water basin, the soil is piled to the desired level right away, saving us a lot of cement. The external shape is pegged out with small posts onto which we nail twenty centimeter broad strips of presswood. These five millimeter thick presswood sheets are very pliable, and by using them the basin can be given any shape we desire.

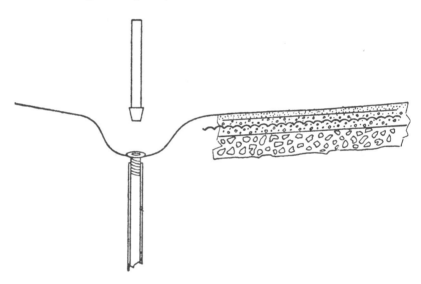

Diagram of the bottom and drain pipe construction for the turtle pond. The arrangement of different substrates shown here provides the best bottom which is least subject to erosion. The area near the drain pipe must have at least a 5% gradient.

The external walls of our construction are formed and concreted to the water basin in one operation. Then we cover the whole surface with a ten - centimeter deep layer of coarse broken stone which is rammed, and on top of this we put a sheet of

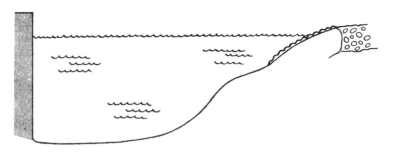

Unless the sides of the pond slope slightly, the turtles will be unable to leave the water to bask. If the sloped side, or at least a part of it, is covered with concrete and given a "ripple" finish, the turtles will find it easier still to bask on shore.

structural steel material which has to fit accurately and has been bent to shape. The ready mixed concrete must not be runny. The gravel we use should preferably be of a granulation from 0 to 30. When we have put in the concrete we ram it and make sure the structural steel mat is lying in the middle of the concrete layer. After 24 hours the cement has set enough for us to be able to apply a two‑centimeter thick layer of flush plaster. Sharp corners and angles are rounded off with the bottom part of a bottle. All round the drain hole we leave a pocket with a depth of ten centimeters and a diameter of twenty to thirty centimeters. The whole bottom surface of the basin has to slope sufficiently for the dirty water to run off quickly.

A water conduit leading into the pond saves us a lot of work. The tap is fitted at the top part of one outside wall so that we can reach it easily when standing in the empty basin. It should be possible to connect a garden hose to the tap. The outlet should be fitted in such a way that the stand pipe is easy to get at from the outside.

The rising part of the basin near the edges is forever covered in algae and becomes so slippery that the animals are barely able to get ashore. This can be prevented by the following construction. 24 hours after applying the coat of flush plaster, mix half a bucket of cement with water to form a thick pulp. Stir this with a trowel until all the lumps of dry cement have dissolved. A

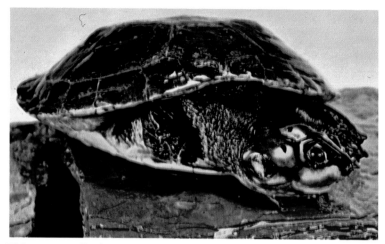

This young *Podocnemis expansa* may be one of the last of a dying breed. This species has been so heavily exploited that many populations are extinct or nearly so. Photo by Dr. Herbert R. Axelrod.

Hatchlings of the various species of sea turtles are sometimes offered for sale. Because of the dangerously reduced sea turtle populations and the fact that most captive sea turtle young will not survive without extraordinary care, avoid the temptation to buy them. Photo of loggerhead turtle *(Caretta caretta)* by D. Faulkner.

Although some species of *Gopherus* are still locally common, gopher tortoises should not be kept as pets. The eastern gopher tortoise *(Gopherus polyphemus*, above) is now rare where a few years ago it was common. No one knows how many Bolson tortoises *(Gopherus flavomarginatus*, below) are left, but there are certainly not many. Photos by P. C. H. Pritchard.

one-centimeter thick layer of this pulp is applied to the slanting side of the basin. The pulp has to be so thick that it does not run. Pull a hard old broom or a bundle of twigs through the freshly applied cement, making small horizontal elevations, rather like the ripplemarks on a sandy seashore, which will later give support to the animals when they climb out of the water. However, the edges of these "waves" would be too sharp for the delicate feet of the turtles, and the plastron is delicate too and could get damaged. Therefore, round off the edges, using a soft brush or a strong paint brush. About one hour after applying the cement, carefully go over the projections with the wet brush. In this way the cement, which is still soft, is rounded off evenly. If this is done properly and gently, the desired structure will not be destroyed.

Particularly suitable for the outside walls are plastic sheeting and wire-reinforced glass. How these sheets are built in and fastened has already been described in connection with the building of an outdoor terrarium for land tortoises. An outside wall made of cement looks clumsy and unattractive, and to use natural stones is not advisable either since, being naturally rough and uneven, they make it only too easy for the animals to climb over the walls. All the walls and corners have to be smooth and must not offer any support. Aquatic turtles are good climbers, and even bushes, shrubs, and over-leaning branches are used as ladders by them.

DECORATING THE POOL

When planting the land part of the pool, make sure that a certain distance is maintained between walls and plants. The bushes must also be pruned regularly. Cover the land part with grass sods or with irregularly shaped tiles of natural stone.

Both practical and attractive is the imitation of a river bank or the shore of a lake. Here the water basin takes up two-thirds of the whole surface and the remaining third is made to look like a sandy shore. We start at the edge of the basin and dig ten centimeters deep into the land part so that the excavated area rises gradually towards the back. The soil we have dug up is transferred to the background of the pond and then levelled. In this way we get a gently sloping river bank. Now we bury three to four large flower pots into which we can put plants later on. At the highest point, in the furthest corner of the land part, build a small frame of about 60 by 60 centimeters from a few stones and a little cement. This frame is filled with a mixture of peat and sand (one part peat and two parts fine sand). Here the animals will later go to lay their eggs.

Finally, put in a ten-centimeter layer of gravel, preferably the kind used for garden paths, with a granulation of ten to fifteen millimeters. Never use sharp-edged, machine-broken gravel, but always natural rounded pit or river gravel. To make our landscape look more attractive, we put several rounded pebbles, thirty to fifty centimeters in size, on top of the gravel. These smooth stones can be found in almost any fast running brook or river, in the river bed or on the shore.

TEMPERATURES

An outdoor terrarium where the land part has been covered with a thick layer of gravel is much warmer than a terrarium with grass. This is because the gravel cover stores far more heat when the sun is shining on it, and this heat is slowly given off again over-night. This source of heat can be exploited particularly well if we cover the terrarium with a plastic sheet after sun set. I recorded the temperatures over a period of several weeks and found that in a terrarium where the land part is lined with a layer of gravel the temperatures are by about five to eight degrees higher than they are in a grassy terrarium. The recordings were regularly carried out at seven o'clock in the morning.

During the warm summer months we can keep tropical species in the outdoor terrarium, too; but when it rains, or on days with little sun, we have to take them out again, unless we prefer to

All giant tortoises are rare and should not be kept by individuals. Their reproductive rate is so low that many, such as this saddleback tortoise from the Galapagos *(Geochelone elephantopus ephippium)*, are really extinct species waiting for the last aged survivors to die. Photo by P. C. H. Pritchard at the Bronx Zoo.

The eastern United States species of wood turtles, genus *Clemmys*, are all endangered. The spotted turtle *(Clemmys guttata)* is one of the most attractive little turtles in the northeast, and it is rapidly becoming rare. Photo by P. C. H. Pritchard.

leave them outdoors and replace the missing warmth of the sun with two infrared ray lamps over the water and a heating cable in the water. It goes without saying that the terrarium is kept covered if we supply it with additional heating. When using electric heaters outdoors, we have to be careful. The instruments must be grounded. Lamps and connections must be protected against rain and damp.

Many aquatic turtles like to bask in the sun for hours, and they prefer to do this in the immediate proximity of the water so that they can plunge into it the moment they feel they are in danger. For small turtles, put in an island made of ornamental cork. Larger animals, however, appreciate a thickish, preferably flattened, tree trunk provided with a few branches. Put part of this tree trunk on the shore and anchor it there with strong screws and two flat iron bars knocked into the ground. The trunk should be lying at an angle so that half of it is below the water surface; this makes it easier for the animals to climb out. Saw through the length of the trunk, i.e. from the part that is lying on the shore to where it is immersed at the edge of the water basin. To make the whole design look natural, do not use absolutely straight tree trunks, but choose one that is crooked and flattened and has got thick branches, if possible.

PLANTS

What plants do we use? This depends primarily on whether we have a bright room available, safe from frost, for the storage of foreign and non-perennial varieties, since we want to make sure our plants get through the winter unharmed. Particularly well suited and very decorative is the dwarf palm, *Chamerops humilis,* which will survive the winter at a temperature of 3 - 5° C, or the agave, *Agave americana,* whose bright fancy varieties add some color to the scenery. To those who wish to plant conifers I recommend the cedars, with their broad growth. The stunted form of the Japanese cedar, *Cryptomeria japonica,* also is very suitable.

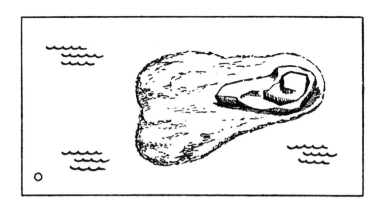

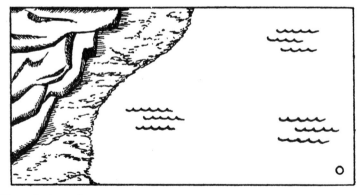

The relation of the land area to the water area can be designed to suit the individual pond and its inhabitants. An island is often best for nervous species, while land areas along the sides make it easier to recapture diseased turtles or those that need special attention.

The tufted Spanish bayonet, *Yucca aloifolia,* keeps quite well, and so does *Aloe arborescens.*

All around the plants the pots are covered with flat stones on top of which we then put gravel. In this way we prevent the tortoises from scratching out the earth and damaging the roots of the plants.

CARE AND CLEANING

The water basin is cleaned as required. But not all the algae should be removed when we do this. Many turtles graze on tender algae and, over and above that, the algae help greatly to keep the water clear. The very coarse dirt gathers around the drain pipe in the depression provided for it; by lifting the drain pipe for a moment in the morning and at night it can easily be removed without much water being lost.

How long can turtles from warmer countries be left in the outdoor pool? This depends entirely on the weather. The temperature is recorded every morning in any case. Delicate species, those requiring plenty of warmth, and young animals of all species should be taken out of the outdoor enclosure as soon as the temperature drops below 18° C. Large animals, including those from tropical zones, can stay outside until the temperature falls to below 16° C, provided they are strong and well nourished. I have applied this rule of thumb for many years and never observed any animals suffering from colds or chills.

Often we still get warm, sunny days in late fall which we should utilize. If the weather permits, the transfer to the indoor terrarium is postponed for several weeks. But in that case we have to assist matters a little at night by using an infrared lamp.

Everyone who has kept turtles knows how good it is for the health of the animals to be kept outdoors in the summer. They leave their outdoor terrarium strong and heavy. It is only when they have all been transferred to the indoor terrarium that we realize how much they have grown; in spring they still had sufficient room and swimming space and now, in autumn, conditions seem to be rather cramped. So sometime soon there comes the day when we are forced to reduce our stock or to exchange the biggest animals for young animals.

Non-perennial plants are taken out of the enclosure before the first frosts set in. During the winter keep them in rooms which are safe from frost but bright. Just before winter, the water basin is cleaned thoroughly one more time. When the water has run off, put a piece of fine mesh netting over the drain and fill the whole basin with dry leaves. Finally everything is covered with plastic sheeting or roofing paper. Electrical equipment and the drain pipe are taken indoors. The water supply to the terrarium is turned off.

Next spring the leaves are taken out first. Then we make a plug from fine wire netting which fits exactly into the opening of the drain. For, first of all we want to wash the gravel from the land part in the water basin and for that the drain pipe would be in the way. The wire stopper prevents the pebbles from going down the drain. Now all the gravel is shovelled into the water basin and treated with a strong water jet and a scrubbing brush. The soil that we have provided for egg-laying is loosened up and added to if necessary.

PRECAUTIONS

In conclusion, there are two great dangers I have to point out.

1. Temperature recordings must never be carried out with an unprotected glass thermometer. Turtles are always hungry and greedy and will try to snatch it under the assumption that everything dipped into their basin is edible. The thin glass tube breaks easily and, even if the small pieces are not swallowed, they can cause severe injuries.

2. It is true that a newly cemented water basin can be filled with water after three days, for by then the cement is hard. But

it only sets properly after 28 days and until then it gives off substances which cause dangerous, often fatal, skin damage to the animals. We have to make sure, therefore, that a newly built water basin is watered for at least 14 days (whereby the walls are scrubbed from time to time and the water is changed) before the animals are put in.

INDOOR QUARTERS

Turtles are aquatic animals and can, in many ways, be treated the same as fish. The major differences are that they must get to the surface to breathe, they usually require some type of basking area, and they foul their water more.

Large turtles, those over eight or nine inches long, are generally too large and active to be kept in indoor aquaria. Perhaps you can fix a plastic wading pool or something similar for them. Our discussion will be limited to turtles less than eight inches long. Since juvenile red-ears and cooters are the most commonly kept turtles, their housing accommodations will be considered first.

CLEAN WATER

Baby cooters should not be kept in smaller than 5-gallon tanks, nor should they be crowded in larger tanks. Allow about one square foot of surface area for each turtle if the animal is less than four inches long. Less than this will lead to rapid fouling of the water. Turtles are famous for passing mostly undigested food within a few hours of eating it, so arrangements must be made for either changing the water every few days or for filtering the tank. With a five-gallon tank containing only four or five inches of water, water changes every other day are not too time consuming. If your time is limited, use one of the many different types of filters available at your pet shop. All require an air pump in order to operate, so you must also buy one of these;

69

small diaphragm pumps are very inexpensive. If you get an underground filter, you must use gravel on the bottom of the tank. This is someting of a nuisance, since you will have to clean out the gravel every few weeks (turtles are much messier than fish), so one of the small self-contained inside filters is your best bet. Just make sure that it will operate in only a few inches of water.

If you wish to spend the least possible time cleaning up after your pets, feed them in a separate tray or bowl of water and let them stay there for two or three hours after eating. Most undigested and digested food remains are passed within this period, so there will be relatively little fouling of the tank water.

BASKING

To remain healthy, your turtle needs to bask often. Placing the tank in the sunlight can be dangerous. Even though the natural light is probably best for the turtle, the cold drafts usually associated with windows may cause pneumonia. Also, turtles basking in any light, natural or artificial, require a hiding place when the light becomes too bright. The best method is to use a 40 to 60 watt incandescent bulb in a reflector. Suspended about a foot above the basking area, this will provide sufficient heat and light to keep your pets healthy. The reflector will prevent the whole tank from being exposed to the light, so large cool areas will be left for the turtles to retreat to.

Aquariums must either be kept in a warm room (warm enough to maintain a *water* temperature of 75° F), or a heater must be used. Since tanks for baby cooters usually contain only a few inches of water, suspended aquarium heaters are hard to use. They will work, though inefficiently, if put into a jar full of water; the jar is then placed in the tank. Disadvantages of this system are obvious: the jar becomes very warm before the tank water even starts to warm up, so the water in the jar evaporates rapidly and must be replaced often. If the jar tips over, you might end up with scalded turtles. The best solution is to use a sub-merged heater with a separate thermostat; these are more expensive than suspended heaters, but are cheaper to operate and safer under such conditions.

The basking platform can be of any type of material, as long as it is waterproof and not too rough for the plastrons. In a tank with only a few inches of water, large rocks or pieces of cork may be used. The only requirement is that the turtles be able to leave the water and dry completely, including the plastron. If it is not feasible to build a sloping basking board of wood or plastic, one can be suspended from the sides of the tank.

LARGER TURTLES

Larger turtles are more difficult to house, since they require more swimming room and are even dirtier than baby turtles. A twenty to fifty gallon tank should handle several medium-sized specimens with ease, as long as they are given sufficient basking room. A large power filter is almost a must for such an aquarium if it is to remain clean. With large turtles, care must be taken that any piece of equipment inside the tank, such as thermometers and heaters, is adequately protected from jaws, legs, and turtle shell. Large water turtles can be quite vicious with anything they believe might be edible — and they think everything is food.

CHAPTER SEVEN.   CARE AND FEEDING OF AQUATIC TURTLES

GROWTH SUPPLEMENTS

ULTRAVIOLET

If we have to keep our aquatic turtles in the indoor terrarium all the year round, we have to treat them with an ultraviolet lamp at least two to three times a week. The lamp is hung up over the terrarium at a distance of 80 centimeters. Three to five minutes of treatment per session are sufficient. It is much better to irradiate the terrarium more frequently for five minutes than to do it just once or twice a week and then for longer.

CALCIUM

Young animals which are still growing have to be given calcium at regular intervals. This is unnecessary only if we feed them mainly on small fishes or can offer them plenty of aquatic snails. Animals almost exclusively fed on muscle meat require half a tablet of calcium supplement once a week. The tablet is crushed in a small mortar and mixed with two cubic centimeters of water so that a cloudy suspension of the very smallest particles is formed. This suspension may be drawn up with a syringe and with a broad cannula injected into an earthworm or mealworm. The worm is then fed to the turtles immediately.

If we have got a fairly large stock of turtles it would be an advantage to use a liquid calcium preparation. There are calcium bottles with rubber seals which will keep for several weeks when stored cool, even if they have already been started. Preparations in ampoules are very good, too, but for our purposes they are too expensive.

The calcium solution can, of course, also be injected into a strip of meat. For this the meat is cut along the fibers. The same method — injecting into pieces of food — is applied when the animals are given two drops of vitamins once a week. This preparation contains all the vital vitamins, and it should be given regularly. Unfortunately the preparation has such a strong odor that the animals refuse to take it. But if we inject it into a worm they do not notice it and we can give this multi-vitamin preparation to them at regular intervals.

VARIED DIET

It would be completely wrong to feed our pets on nothing but the meat of warm-blooded animals and on vitamins: they would soon come to suffer from deficiency diseases. We have to make sure they get a varied diet. Nor is this difficult, since nature provides us with everything a turtle stomach appreciates. Let us see what a turtle menu can look like during the different seasons.

In spring we find large quantities of tadpoles and newts, as well as all sorts of water beetles, in every pool. In the garden we can gather earthworms, caterpillars, and snails; on the edge of the forest we collect beetles, crickets, and small grasshoppers. For turtle babies, too, the larder is full in spring. In the ponds we find large water fleas, mosquito larvae, and caddis worms, the larvae of caddis flies; in brooks, tubifex worms and water fleas; and in the garden and on meadows, flies and moths.

In summer we catch small frogs, the larvae of dragonflies, large water beetles, butterflies, earthworms, crickets, and small

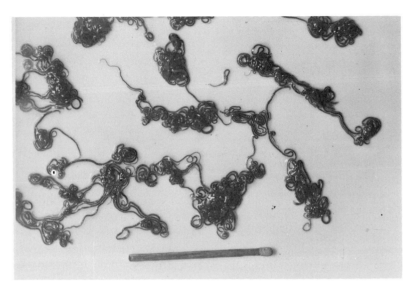

Worms are often the best foods available for water turtles. Tubifex worms (above) can be collected from clean lakes (be sure to wash them before feeding), bought from the pet store, or obtained in freeze-dried form. Earthworms (below) are easily collected after heavy rains or may be bought from sporting goods dealers. The small worms are usually preferred. Photos by G. J. M. Timmerman (above) and P. Imgrund (below).

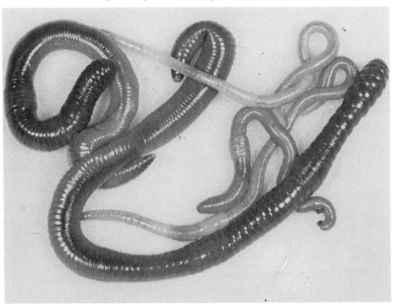

Snails are often enjoyed by many species of turtles. Try to get species which have thin shells and are small in size. Photo by Knaack.

Although garden slugs of various types are common, few animals will eat them. Try drowning a few in warm water and washing off the mucous before feeding. Photo by P. Imgrund.

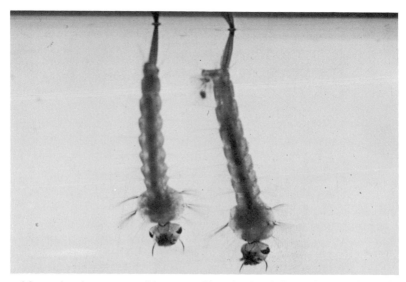

Mosquito larvae provide a readily obtained food for small and medium-sized turtles. They also store well when frozen. Do not leave living larvae in the turtle tank, or you will soon have mosquitoes flying around. Photo by Knaack.

Bloodworms (larvae of chironomid midges) are not only excellent fish food, but also very popular with young or small turtles. Photo by Knaack.

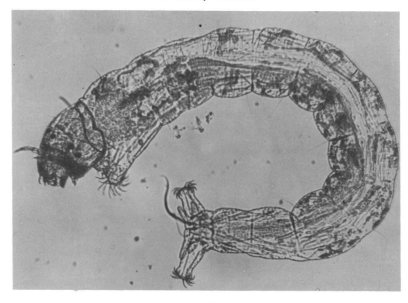

grasshoppers (the big green katydids are quite popular, too), and dig for the fat larvae of June beetles. On rainy days we collect slugs and land snails. In streams and ponds we look for water snails and small clams. The young animals can eat water fleas, mosquito larvae, tubifex, flies and their larvae, cockroaches, isopods, centipedes, earwigs, small grasshoppers and moths during the summer, and they will eagerly take chopped earthworms as well.

In the autumn collect worms, white grubs, snails, and beetles in the garden and in the compost heap. On the edge of the wood there are still grasshoppers and spiders, in the pond young frogs, snails, large water beetles and their larvae. In the forest we can gather old mushrooms containing plenty of grubs and small organisms. The pool will still be full of fat beetles, *Daphnia,* mosquito larvae, and tubifex, and our fly trap in the garden or at the kitchen window will still be well stocked.

In winter, feeding becomes a little more difficult, but even then it can still be varied. In brooks and ponds, even below the ice, we will find water fleas, the larvae of caddis flies, mosquito larvae, and tubifex. In summer we started a culture of crickets or migratory locusts which will now provide sufficient food animals. Earthworms gathered during the autumn have multiplied inside their box in the cool cellar, which means we have large numbers of very small worms for the young turtles. Now the mealworm culture we have left undisturbed the whole summer has to be used, too. If all this is still not enough to satisfy all the animals, let them have frozen clams or pond snails, meat, horse or beef heart and liver. Vegetable food such as aquatic plants and tender lettuce should also be offered regularly.

Small freshwater fishes are difficult to get, unless we culture them ourselves. It is important, however, that small turtles are given some of this highly nutritious food at regular intervals. We might be lucky if we ask professional fishermen, fishing clubs, and pond owners.

CHAPTER EIGHT. COMMON TURTLES

Of the many known aquatic turtles, I only want to mention those that are offered on the market most frequently. Information on the other species, as well as the tortoises, can be found in Pritchard's *Living Turtles of the World,* TFH Publications.

EUROPEAN POND TURTLE

The European pond turtle is *Emys orbicularis* and occurs throughout much of Europe. In the past it used to be encountered frequently, but today — owing to progressive civilization — it has become very rare. The draining of marshes and the control of rivers have limited its living space considerably. In the few areas where it is still possible for it to live it is ruthlessly hunted by man, the most dangerous of its enemies. It is very widely distributed over the whole of southern Europe and parts of central Europe to the Far East. In Albania and Italy the pond turtle is still so common that it can be exported in large numbers every year.

A few years ago I made a short research trip to the Po area, the center of Italian rice cultivation. It was late in summer and I was able to walk around several rice fields undisturbed. No matter where I went and into what direction, I saw the same picture everywhere — numerous pond tortoises in all sizes were lying in the sun on the edge of pools and noiselessly slipped into the water when I approached. They allowed me to come fairly close, but when I was less than five meters away from them, they slipped into the water and disappeared in the muddy bottom.

In these pools the animals find food in plenty. Fairly large shoals of small whitings glide through the water, pond frogs in all sizes float croaking on the surface. But for the very small turtles there is adequate food of convenient size, too: *Daphnia,* aquatic and terrestrial insects, worms, mosquito larvae — all the delicacies a turtle stomach appreciates.

The ponds in the rice field area are interconnected by a canal system. In this way the desired water level is maintained. The water which has been lost through evaporation is constantly being replaced with new water from the river nearby. New shoals of fish keep arriving in the ponds via these canals, and it is a great pleasure to discover a turtle paradise in an area with so much farming. From time to time, however, the rice farmers dredge some of the turtles out of the mud with large rakes, pack them into boxes and baskets, and the buyers then despatch them into every part of the world.

The European pond turtle is easy to keep in captivity. Its flattened carapace reaches a length of 20 centimeters. The basic color of the carapace is blackish green, and it is speckled with rows of yellow spots. These yellow spots are found on the legs and the head as well. Markings and basic coloration vary greatly; usually the animals living in the south are slightly lighter in color than those hailing from northern regions.

Sexually mature animals will propagate in the outdoor terrarium, too. They mate in spring, usually in May. During copulation the male attaches itself to the back of the female and is carried around by her. Sometimes the animals mate on the shore and sometimes in the water. At the end of May, in the evening hours, the gravid female leaves the water and looks for a suitable place to bury its eggs. When a place has been found, the animal digs a hole with its hind legs and lays 9 to 15 eggs. The small cavity has a diameter of 10 to 15 centimeters and a depth of 6 to 8 centimeters. The soft shells of the eggs

The European pond turtle often appears on the lists of dealers. Although not very attractive turtles, they are said to be very intelligent and personable. Photo by P. C. H. Pritchard.

quickly grow hard in the air. Finally the animal carefully fills in the hole again, levels it with the plastron and flattens it. After this hard work the female goes back into the water and forgets about the offspring, leaving everything to Nature. The young hatch at the end of August or the beginning of September. To rear them will, however, only succeed in the heated terrarium, since the winter nights are far too cool for such delicate young animals to grow well.

The newly hatched young have to be isolated from the adult turtles, since the old ones regard the young as a very welcome food. In the middle of August, therefore, put a small wooden frame, lined with fine wire netting, over the cavity with the eggs. At night the frame is covered with a cloth. Under no circumstances must the eggs be taken out of the ground at this advanced stage of development, for if their position were to be changed by us the young would die. How to raise the young will be described in a later chapter.

SPANISH TURTLE

This turtle attains a size of up to 20 centimeters. Its home is North Africa and the Iberian peninsula. The green to brown carapace is covered with orange spots, and the limbs and neck have yellowish white, or yellow-orange, stripes.

Unfortunately this attractive turtle, which is easy to keep, is rarely imported. The same goes for its relative, *Clemmys caspica rivulata,* which occurs in Albania, southern Yugoslavia, Greece, Bulgaria, and parts of Turkey. The gray-green background color of its carapace is decorated with white net-like markings. Neck and limbs show grayish white stripes.

The Spanish turtle (often called the Moorish turtle) is perhaps best called by its scientific name, *Clemmys caspica.* The several subspecies differ in color, but the juveniles are all quite attractive. Photo by R. J. Church.

ASIATIC ROOFED TURTLE

Kachuga tecta tecta is one of the most beautiful and brilliantly colored aquatic turtles, with its colorfulness surpassing even the American cooters. It lives in the Ganges and Indus River regions of India and Pakistan. The high, roof-shaped carapace is olive brown in color, in youth pale green. The dorsal keel is formed by reddish humps with a black margin. The plastron is orangish yellow to red with large black patches.

The crown of the head is dark brown, the back of the head and the jaws are bright red, the neck is gray green with yellow stripes, and the legs are of the same color but are speckled instead of striped.

The animal needs plenty of warmth. To keep it is not difficult as long the high warmth requirements can be satisfied. *Kachuga tecta tecta* feeds almost exclusively on plants. All sorts of aquatic plants are eaten, but also lettuce, cabbage, dandelion, and young shoots of the spiderwort *(Tradescantia)*. For variety, offer a little meat cut into strips as well, and earthworms, mealworms, grasshoppers, fish, slugs, and water insects.

Very young animals like mosquito larvae, tubifex, and water fleas very much, but take vegetable food, too. For many years I owned a fully-grown male which had a preference for pieces of banana, pears, strawberries, but also ate clams and fish. Occasionally it even took raisins which had been soaked in water for 24 hours.

For this turtle we need large aquaria, as it is a very good swimmer and attains the considerable length of 25 centimeters.

REEVES' TURTLE

Reeves' turtle, *Chinemys reevesi,* only grows to a size of 12 centimeters, but is very lively and long-lived. It is an ideal pet which is commonly offered on the market. It lives in southeast China, in Korea, Japan, and the Philippines. The carapace is light brown with yellow seams, and there are three ridges or keels that run longitudinally along the carapace. Yellow longitudinal lines and spots decorate the soft parts of the body. Completely black animals are extremely rare and are said to occur only in China.

Reeves' turtle *(Chinemys reevesi)* is commonly imported as hatchlings. Photo by R. J. Church.

Reeves' turtle is particularly well suited for the outdoor terrarium, as it is active and lively even on cool days. In summer it sometimes buries itself and only returns to the water after days or weeks. Feeding is no problem: it eats everything that other aquatic turtles like, too, especially earthworms and tadpoles.

RED-EARED TURTLE

This, the most familiar of the pet turtles, needs no description. It is found from Georgia west and north to Texas and Ohio, and is the common turtle of these areas. *Pseudemys scripta elegans* and *P. s. scripta* can be told from the other cooters sold in pet shops by the color pattern of the carapace. In both young and older specimens the large scutes of the carapace have a broad light vertical line. Young of this, as well as most aquatic turtles, love freeze-dried tubifex worms.

The two sliders most likely to be found in pet shops: *Pseudemys scripta elegans,* the red-ear (above) and *Pseudemys floridana* subspecies, the Florida cooter (below). Notice that in *P. floridana* all the lines on the head are relatively narrow. In *Pseudemys scripta* (all the subspecies commonly sold) the line behind the eye is very broad and often brightly colored: red in *s. elegans* and *s. callirostris*, or a yellow blotch in *scripta scripta.* Photos by R. J. Church.

YELLOW-BELLIED TURTLE

Like the red-eared, but with a large yellow blotch behind the eye, and no red. Found along the Atlantic Coast from northern Florida to North Carolina, it is known to science as *Pseudemys scripta scripta.*

CUMBERLAND TURTLE

This subspecies, *Pseudemys scripta troosti,* is practically identical with the red-eared, but the stripes on the head are all yellow. These three subspecies intergrade over a wide area, and occasionally turtles cannot be easily placed in any subspecies.

COLOMBIAN COOTER

Although a subspecies of the yellow-bellied turtle, the Colombian cooter, *Pseudemys scripta callirostris,* more closely resembles the Florida cooter and its relatives. Each large scute of the carapace is marked with a "C"-shaped yellow line enclosing a black spot, and the underside of the head and chin are yellow with numerous open black circles, giving the effect of a few large yellow spots. There is, however, a red or bright orange line back from the eye, as in the red-eared turtle. As its common name indicates, this species is found in northern Colombia and Venezuela. It is the only Central or South American cooter commonly imported.

FLORIDA COOTERS

Pseudemys floridana and subspecies related to it form one of the most confusing groups of the genus. Several of the eight subspecies show up in shipments of red-eared turtles from time to time and can be treated similarly. The major problem is finding out just what you have. These turtles usually have a "C"-shaped marking on each of the large scutes of the carapace, and several other light and dark connected lines on each scute. There is usually no red in the head pattern, and if there is, there is more than one such line on each side of the head. Florida cooters range over most of the southern United States, and include the largest (16 inches) form of the genus in this country. It is almost a waste of time trying to identify the subspecies unless you know exactly where they originated. All are similar in body form and color, so just call them *Pseudemys floridana.*

In addition to the species mentioned above, there are several others which are found in the West Indies, Central, and South America. These are very hard to identify, and are very rarely imported. However, one or more species may rarely show up in almost any lot of red-ears you happen to examine. Red-bellied turtles *(Pseudemys rubriventris* and relatives) may also be seen for sale in the Middle Atlantic states, where they occur naturally. Red-bellies have, as the name implies, much red on the shell and red lines on the head.

COOTERS IN GENERAL

The cooters grow rapidly and live up to 20 years. For best results, they should be kept in filtered tanks or outdoor pools, be well fed, and be kept warm. Young turtles need a lot of calcium in their diet for good shell formation. Never paint the shell, as this prevents growth and eventually causes death. These are the turtles which have been repeatedly tied in with *Salmonella* incidents in children, so be careful to never place them near food, wash them in the kitchen sink, or place them or their water near the mouth. This applies especially to children, whose low body weight make them very prone to severe attacks of the disease. Careful attention to cleanliness for a few weeks after purchasing, followed by care not to overfeed, will prevent most chances of contamination. More about *Salmonella* later.

Millions of red-eared turtles have died at the hands of children and adults who either bought the turtles as playthings or were misinformed. Turtles are living animals, not inanimate objects; they live only when cared for; they die when neglected. "Turtle food" consisting of dried flies and ant eggs or pupae does not provide enough nutrients to enable a young turtle to survive, no matter what the label or dealer says. It should be given only in small quantities, and only as a "treat." Freeze-dried tubifex worms, sardines, excess guppies or goldfish, and fresh green vegetables will provide a balanced diet.

PAINTED TURTLE

Closely related to the red-ears and cooters is the painted turtle, *Chrysemys picta*. In fact, the two genera are so similar that some scientists want to place the cooters in the same genus *(Chry-*

The bright red dorsal stripe of juvenile southern painted turtles set them off from all other North American turtles. Photo by R. J. Church.

semys) as the painted turtle. As we will use it here, however, *Chrysemys* has only one species, but it is widely distributed over all of the eastern and northwestern United States. There are four subspecies recognized, but all are basically similar. These are low-shelled turtles, with yellow-striped heads, sometimes with yellow spots as well, and bright red markings either on the marginals (the square scutes which form a circle around the carapace) or on the plastron. One subspecies even has a bright red line down the middle of the back!

At one time painted turtles were commonly sold as pets, but this is not generally true now. Most specimens you see in pet shops will be locally collected turtles which will adapt well to your tank.

They can be treated like cooters, but are almost completely carnivorous, eating fish, insects, snails, and almost any other living or freshly killed food. Occasionally a little vegetable matter will be taken.

MAP TURTLES

The map turtles include some of the most attractive (in a subdued way), uncommon, and delicate turtles to be found in the United States. There are at least twelve described species and subspecies, but only two are ever available in any quantity. All the species are built along the same line: round to oval carapace with a mid-dorsal keel which, in juveniles and males, appears tooth-like; the marginals between the hind legs come to points; the skin is dark, marked with yellow lines, and there is usually at least one yellow spot behind the eye; and the carapace is brownish with yellow or orange lines or circles.

The common map turtle *(Graptemys geographica)* is the most northern species, being found over most of the middle and eastern United States and north into Canada. It is probably also the species most commonly seen in pet shops. The keel is poorly developed, even in juveniles, but there is a triangular

The Mississippi map turtle *(Graptemys kohni)* is often found mixed with shipments of red-ears. As a rule, the hatchlings of map turtles seldom survive long in captivity. Photo by R. J. Church.

The eastern painted turtle provides a sharp contrast between the dark, nearly black carapace and the red lateral markings. Painted turtles make good pets and adapt well to captivity. Photo by R. J. Church.

yellow spot behind the eye and irregular yellow lines over most of the carapace.

Graptemys kohni, the Mississippi map turtle, is a strongly keeled species easily identified by the comma-like yellow blotch behind the eye; this blotch separates the fine yellow lines from the eye. This is a common species of clean, large rivers and backwaters from Nebraska to Louisiana.

Except for *Graptemys pseudogeographica,* the false map turtle, all the other map turtles are either rare or found only in very limited areas, such as one small river system. The false map turtle is found over much of the central United States, and differs from the common map turtle in its more elongate shape, stronger keel, and fewer yellow lines on the carapace. It occasionally is found with stocks of red-eared turtles. The other species of *Graptemys* are collector's items.

Map turtles are delicate animals which are often choosey about what they eat, and usually die after a few weeks in captivity. Young maps in captivity do not add calcium to their shells, so even if they eat well, they usually die shortly. Adults are mostly carnivorous, eating clams, snails, crayfish, and insect larvae. Some species, however, require at least some plants in their diet. The water must be kept very clean, and the turtles allowed to bask freely.

This is one of the genera of turtles which shows a great amount of difference between the sexes (sexual dimorphism). Males are often half or less of the size of the females (females of most species reach about 10 inches in length, while few males exceed five inches), and keep the juvenile colors and shell shape; females lose much of the color and keeling with age.

DIAMONDBACK TERRAPIN

This turtle of brackish water marshes is more renowed for its gourmet usage than for its value as a pet. When there were more turtles and people had slightly different tastes, diamondbacks were

Since diamondback terrapins are brackish water turtles, their tank water should be kept slightly salty. If kept in fresh water, many specimens develop a deadly fungus within a few weeks. Photo courtesy the American Museum of Natural History.

sold in most coastal fish markets and fetched a good price. Now there are seldom enough turtles at any one spot to permit commercial harvesting, and people prefer to keep turtles instead of eating them. The several similar subspecies of the diamondback range along the Atlantic and Gulf coasts of the United States.

Diamondbacks are easily identified by the greatly ridged shell, the ridges forming concentric circles on each scute. The skin color is usually a bluish gray, with black spots. The color of the carapace and plastron varies with locality, as do details of body color and pattern. These turtles must be kept in water containing a little salt or they will rapidly develop a deadly growth of fungus. Feed them on snails and fish. The scientific name of the diamondback terrapin is *Malaclemys terrapin.*

AMBOINA BOX TURTLE

The Amboina or Malayan box turtle, *Cuora amboinensis*, which reaches a length of 20 centimeters, hails from Indochina,

Malaya, Indonesia and the Philippines. Adapted to a warm climate, it becomes active only at temperatures within the range of 25 to 28° C. The hemispherical carapace reminds one of that of a land tortoise, but the front and rear lobes of the plastron are movable. The plastron is yellow with large black spots, and the carapace is brown. Neck and head are brown on top, with two yellow longitudinal lines running along the sides and meeting at the snout. This turtle is a very good swimmer and spends most of its time in the water. When it goes ashore it likes to bury itself several centimeters deep in the sand. Apart from fish, mussels, meat, and worms, it also likes insects, but its main diet consists of lettuce and fruits, particularly bananas.

Cuora trifasciata, a box turtle from southern China and northern Indochina, is seldom available. Owing to its bright yellow head framed by two black stripes going through the eyes, it is sometimes called the "little yellow-head." The carapace has three keels and, running parallel to them, three black longitudinal stripes. The dark brown plastron is framed with yellow. The soft parts and the inner margins of the carapace are salmon red. Food habits are the same as those of *Cuora amboinensis.*

MUD TURTLES

If you want to start off with a cheap, hardy, easily kept species of water turtle, one of the mud turtles (genus *Kinosternon)* is just the thing for you. There are over a dozen species of these turtles, all very similar in size, shape, and color, distributed over much of North, Central, and South America. They are primitive turtles with large heads, strong jaws, an elongate, slightly flattened or low-keeled carapace, and a small plastron. Few species exceed six inches in length. Closely related to the much larger snapping turtles (both are sometimes placed in the family Chelydridae, although mud turtles and their close relatives are usually placed in the separate family Kinosternidae), they have much the same disposition when first captured: the strong jaws on the flexible neck try to bite anything that comes too close. Fortunately,

Cuora, although unrelated to the American box turtles, has developed a similar hinge on the anterior part of the plastron. The prominent concave area in the back half of the plastron indicates that the specimen is a male. This concavity is also present in the males of many other turtles. Photo of *C. amboinensis* by G. Marcuse.

The mud turtles *(Kinosternon)* are primitive animals often said to be related to the snapping turtles. They are very hard to identify to species. Photo by G. Marcuse.

however, they soon calm down and adjust to the tank. All species are carnivores, and especially enjoy fresh fish, crayfish, insect larvae, and any similar tidbits.

Because they are not truly aquatic, it is best to keep them in tanks with only a few inches of water and a place for them to burrow. Mud turtles live up to their name — they are found in stagnant muddy ponds and ditches, often at least partially buried in the soft bottom. Temperatures can be warm or moderate, as long as the water is not allowed to become too cold.

Of the North American species, *Kinosternon subrubrum* is the most common and widely distributed. It has a dark greenish-brown carapace and dark skin with yellow lines or spots on the head and neck. It is found over much of the southern and central United States. There are many other species in Central America, and some in the southwestern United States and northern South America, but they are all very much like *K. subrubrum*. A few are slightly more attractive, with better defined color patterns of blacks, browns, yellows and whites, but none is really pretty. Their principal advantage is that they die hard.

YELLOW-SPOTTED AMAZON TURTLE

In recent years there has been a large influx of this species onto the pet market. Juveniles often appear in numbers and at low prices, and make a welcome addition to any collection of aquatic turtles. This is the only species of side-neck turtle commonly offered for sale — the head is withdrawn by bending the neck to one side rather than into an S-curve. *Podocnemis* is a rather large genus of primitive turtles, known from South America and (!) Madagascar.

The yellow-spotted Amazon turtle, *Podocnemis unifilis,* is similar to a cooter in general body form, but the head is very different because of the large eyes placed high on the head. The carapace is brown, as are the head and limbs; the plastron is gray. Bright yellow marks the edges of the carapace, and six large yellow spots are on each side of the head. In nature this species reaches 12 inches, but only juveniles are commonly seen on the market.

Because of its large, forwardly situated eyes and the short snout, the head of a yellow-spotted Amazon does not look very turtle-like. Adults tend to lose or blur the head pattern. Photo by R. J. Church.

Since it is predominately aquatic, the yellow-spotted Amazon turtle can be treated in much the same fashion as the American cooters. In contrast to the largely carnivorous cooters, however, the Amazons are mostly herbivorous, depending largely on fruit which has dropped into the water. So keep them on a largely vegetable diet; it wouldn't hurt to try a bit of freeze-dried tubifex every once-in-a-while, though. Keep the temperature high and the water clean, as for any other turtle.

Although it is seldom imported, another species of *Podocnemis, P. expansa,* is of interest to us. This very large (to 35 inches) turtle is also an inhabitant of the Amazon (both it and *P. unifilis* are found in the Guianas and Brazil). Besides being an important source of food for the Indians, this species is also heavily preyed upon for its eggs. At one time the turtles came ashore in vast numbers to lay their eggs. Waiting natives then collected as many eggs as possible, and extracted oil from them. Needless to say, this could not go on forever, and today the populations of *Podocnemis expansa* are greatly reduced in numbers. But this has not stopped native hunters from killing the adults, collecting the eggs, and selling the young. It seems likely that in a few years *P. expansa* will become a rare, if not extinct, turtle.

MATAMATA

The only other side-neck turtle likely to be seen in pet shops is the bizarre matamata, *Chelys fimbriata.* This large (18 inches) sluggish turtle is an inhabitant of shallow, stagnant waters in the Guianas and Brazil. There it lies in wait for fish or other prey to pass close by. The mouth is very large, and when opened draws in a large amount of water — and the prey. The mouth is then closed, the water ejected, and the fish eaten.

In order for this type of fishing to be effective, the matamata must blend perfectly with the debris and mud on the bottom of the pool. This it succeeds in doing because of the numerous

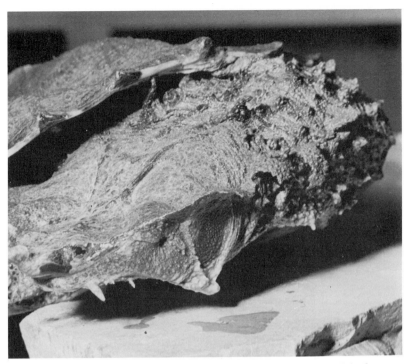

Once you find the eye (extreme left), the rest is easy! This front view of a mata-mata with the neck folded back illustrates the basic character of the side-neck turtles and also emphasizes the bony and fleshy processes on the head of the matamata. Photo by G. Marcuse.

warts, bumps, and fringes of various types which ornament the head and neck. The head is very wide, to accomodate the large mouth, and ends in a long, flexible snout. The snout allows the matamata to breath from below the shallow water without having to move.

As you might guess, such an unusual and large turtle is not often seen in pet shops. When it is imported, however, you can expect to pay a high price for even young specimens. They should be housed in large tanks with a suitable bottom, and do best on live food. They are interesting as an exhibit, but are not exactly the type of turtle one can stroke on the head and feed from the hand.

AMERICAN SOFT-SHELLED TURTLES

The soft-shells are a small world-wide family of very unusual turtles. They are highly specialized, and have reduced most of the boney carapace and plastron which usually signify "turtles" to the average hobbyist. Instead of scutes, the flat carapace is covered with a thick, leathery skin, often roughened, which is highly flexible. The feet are broadly webbed, and the head ends in a long snout which somewhat resembles that of an elephant. The eyes are small and often placed toward the end of the head.

Although there are over 25 species in the world, only four occur in North America. One of these is known only from some ponds in Mexico, so it will not be considered further. The other three species are, however, commonly sold in pet shops.

Since these species are similar in their behavior and requirements, they will first be treated together.

Soft-shells are among the most aquatic of the freshwater turtles, and seldom come out to bask in the sun. Their greatly flattened shape and general brownish coloration allow them to bury themselves in the mud or sand of the bottom and wait for food to come their way. Strong jaws and a cat-like speed allow them to catch small fishes and other animals with ease. They also forage at night on various invertebrates, especially crayfishes and snails, and eat plants and carcasses. On the whole, they are omnivores with a leaning toward small animals as food. Feed plenty of living food, such as small crayfish and snails, and supplement the diet with frozen whole fish such as bait minnows and silversides. Fruit is also accepted.

Since they are almost completely aquatic, a large aquarium or tank of some type is necessary for half-grown or adult specimens. Juveniles can be kept in aquaria similar to those for baby cooters. Filtering is a must, as is a soft sand bottom in which the turtles can bury themselves. Basking logs and lights are not usually necessary, as soft-shells seldom are very active during the day. Generally they stay buried in the bottom with only the neck and head sticking out. They can climb, however, so either keep the

The spiny soft-shell *(Trionyx spiniferus)* has a row of tubercles along the front margin of the carapace; these show well in the photo. The long, flexible snout and the carapace without scutes distinguish the soft-shells. Photo by Dr. Herbert R. Axelrod.

water level below the edge of the tank, or cover the tank securely. If basking platforms are provided, they should be smooth so as not to injure the soft plastron.

Large soft-shells pack a wallop, and their bite really hurts, so be careful. Even juveniles can pinch painfully. The claws are sharp and the legs are strong, so be careful when handling any soft-shell.

Fungus can often be a major problem in the keeping of soft-shells. The leathery carapace and plastron are subject to many scratches and abrasions, and heal only slowly. The best remedy is a clean aquarium and treatment of all scratches as soon as they are noticed. Also, if you purchase a soft-shell, be prepared to eventually move it to a larger tank — our smallest species reaches seven inches in length at maturity, and is about as wide as it is long.

The soft-shell found through most of the U.S. is the spiny soft-shell, *Trionyx spiniferus*. It ranges from the Gulf coast of Mexico, throughout the southern United States, and north to

New York and Montana. There are several subspecies, all slightly different in color and degree of spininess. In all the forms, however, there is a distinct ridge in each nostril and usually a group of spines or tubercles on the anterior edge of the carapace. Most subspecies are light brown above, with blackish spots or circles, these sometimes forming one or more black lines which follow the outline of the carapace. Females are larger than males, and generally have an obscure pattern of dark blotches on a slightly lighter background. Two subspecies have a pattern of light spots on a brownish background.

The spiny softshell varies in maximum size from about ten inches to 15 inches, depending on the subspecies. All are typically inhabitants of lakes or larger streams and rivers, although they will occasionally be found in ponds. They have a long life expectency and make interesting, different pets.

The Florida soft-shell, *Trionyx ferox,* is very similar to the spiny soft-shell, but has a different color pattern. In juveniles, the light brown carapace is almost covered with dark brown, squarish blotches. Adults lose most of the pattern with age, and are just very large (18 inches) blotched brown soft-shells. The spines are in the form of large rounded tubercles on the front margin of the carapace. This species is found only in Florida and adjacent Georgia.

Smallest of the American soft-shells is *Trionyx muticus,* the smooth soft-shell. It averages only 6 or 7 inches in length, although exceptional individuals may reach over 12 inches. Totally lacking spines and tubercles on the carapace, it also lacks ridges in the nostrils, making it easy to distinguish from the spiny and Florida soft-shells. The smooth soft-shell is fairly common over a rather large range, being found from South Dakota and Pennsylvania south to Louisiana and Texas. Although it is an omnivore, it eats more animal matter (mostly crayfish and insect larvae) than do the other species. It is more even-tempered than the other species, and makes a better pet. The color is brown with dark dots.

CHAPTER NINE.   TURTLES AND TORTOISES YOU SHOULDN'T KEEP

Although there are over 200 species of turtles known to exist today, there are a very few which either cannot or should not be kept as pets.   Most species are relatively common, adapt to captivity, and are of a size suitable to indoor aquaria or terraria.   A few, however, grow to very large size and are suitable only for display aquaria.   It is probably not worth your while to purchase such a species unless you have the time and facilities to house and care for it properly.   Other species have become relatively rare in recent times, although they are still sold.   By rare I mean that there are very few individuals to be found in the native habitat, not that they seldom appear on dealers' price lists.   Although most of these are attractive and interesting species, the person who cares anything at all for the future of the hobby should not purchase them.

SNAPPING TURTLES

This group of American turtles (family Chelydridae) contains the largest freshwater turtle in the world, the alligator snapping turtle, *Macrochelys temminckii*.   It also contains the large (15 inches, 50 pounds) common snapping turtle, *Chelydra serpentina*. The alligator snapper is found only in the southern United States, but the common snapper is found from Canada to Ecuador.

Not only is their large size a factor against the selection of these turtles as pets (several species in this book are as large as

If you look closely you can see the light-colored "bait" used by alligator snappers, supposedly to attract curious fish. These turtles are too large to be kept in most tanks. Photo by P. C. H. Pritchard.

common snappers), but also their extreme viciousness. Snappers have the well earned reputation of biting at anything that comes in their way. Their gigantic jaws can easily crush a hand or amputate a finger. They can only be recommended if you have an unused swimming pool into which you can throw fish every few days. And what fun is there in such an arrangement?

OTHER LARGE TURTLES

As a general rule, large specimens of any species are to be avoided, especially when they exceed a foot or so in length (this does not apply to tortoises, of course). Large soft-shells are always vicious. Large matamatas require live fish. Adult specimens of various American and Asian freshwater turtles, all similar to the cooters in build and habits, are also unsuitable because of size. If you buy a ten inch cooter, start thinking about what you will do with it in a few years if it grows a few inches.

SEA TURTLES

As a general rule, no sea turtles should be kept by individuals not directly connected to one of the various breeding programs now in operation around the world. Although some sea turtles are still common locally, all are endangered species which cannot stand any more pressure than necessary. Between egg hunters and meat hunters, the mortality is high each year. Add to this the great percentage of hatchling turtles which never even make it a mile off the beach, and you can see why even a few specimens in private tanks are more than the safety of the species can stand.

What? Who would keep a sea turtle? You would be amazed! With modern salt water aquarium equipment, it is now feasible to keep even large turtles in the home. Of course, you might have to pay $50 or $75 for a two-inch hatchling, but they make great

Sea turtles and some sea snakes are the only living reptiles which have become adapted to a marine aquatic existence. But sea turtles must still lay their eggs on land, allowing them to be hunted and slaughtered in great numbers each year. The eggs and young are also collected or are destroyed by predators. Photo by P. C. H. Pritchard.

conversation pieces. And after the turtle dies of malnutrition or crowding, you can always have it stuffed and put over the mantel. If you have the money, don't let your interest in the unusual get the better of you. Don't buy sea turtles; and explain to any dealer that stocks them why such turtles shouldn't be sold.

GOPHER TORTOISES

These purely North American tortoises were once commonly offered for sale in many parts of the southern and southwestern United States. One species, the Florida gopher tortoise, was even used for food. Today, however, man has decimated their populations over large areas of their natural home, and they are often rare where formerly common.

Of the four species, all very similar in color and build, only one *(Gopherus polyphemus)* is found east of the Mississippi River. It is a rather large burrower, reaching a length of 12 inches. Once common from South Carolina to Mississippi, it is now only abundant in a few areas of Florida.. Not only was it used for food and sold as pets, but its habitat was repeatedly burned over or "improved" by man.

The Bolson tortoise, *Gopherus flavomarginatus,* is known from only a few specimens from Mexico. Although it is not uncommon in a few places, it was only discovered in 1959. Whether it is really rare or no one knows how to find it has yet to be determined. This is the largest of the gopher tortoises, and several specimens over 12 inches long are known; there are rumors and stories of tortoises up to 3 feet long, however.

The desert tortoise, *Gopherus agassizi,* of Arizona and New Mexico, and Berlandier's tortoise of southern Texas, are very similar to each other. Both are still locally common, and are now at least partially protected by state law.

There are two main reasons why these tortoises should not be kept by hobbyists. First, their survival is precarious. They grow slowly and mature late, so they also reproduce slowly. Fires, cattle, parking lots, and collectors have already made a

The genus *Gopherus* is the only group of tortoises native to North America, even though there were once several other genera of giant tortoises in that area. *Gopherus polyphemus* (above) and *Gopherus berlandieri* (below) are both still locally common. Photos by R. J. Church.

sizable dent in the populations. Second, the gopher tortoises may look great in a terrarium, but they simply don't live. Something appears to be missing in captivity, and very few people are able to keep the gophers to a ripe old age. They are very delicate, and are subject to pneumonia at the slightest excuse. So do both yourself and the turtle a favor: don't buy it.

WOOD TURTLES

This is a moderately large genus of pretty turtles, and it contains several popular species. Unfortunately, the three species on the Atlantic coast of the United States are either nearly extinct or are declining in numbers. It has been the misfortune of these turtles to live in areas which have been developed by a rapidly growing human population. Areas of New York, New Jersey, and Pennsylvania where once these turtles were common are now large suburbs of even larger cities. The streams are polluted; marshes have been drained. There is little hope that these turtles will survive without our active assistance.

Muhlenberg's turtle, *Clemmys muhlenbergi,* is one of the rarest North American turtles, and also one of the prettiest. It is a small turtle, with a plain brown carapace. The main distinguishing mark is a bright orange blotch on each side of the head behind the eyes. This is a stream and bog species, a type of habitat which is now rare in its Rhode Island to North Carolina range. The future of this turtle is very uncertain. Specimens should be retained only by individuals and institutions actively engaged in trying to breed this species in captivity.

The aquatic spotted turtle, *Clemmys guttata,* and the wood turtle, *Clemmys insculpta,* have long been popular turtles. Both species are still commonly available on dealers' lists, but fetch high prices. Today they are still locally common in a few areas, but changes in the habitat have led to their disappearance from large areas of their former range. It is now illegal to own these species (and other native species) in New York; other states will probably enact similar laws in the near future.

At one time the wood turtles were commonly kept as pets, and owners said they were the most intelligent of the turtles. Now, however, they have become uncommon or rare in most areas. Muhlenberg's turtle (above) has been called the rarest North American turtle; it may become extinct in the next few decades. The wood turtle (below) may still be locally common, but its ownership is outlawed in several states. Photos by R. J. Church.

Few specimens of spotted turtle *(Clemmys guttata)* are as heavily spotted as this one. This species is more aquatic than the other eastern *Clemmys,* and it is also more common. Photo courtesy of the American Museum of Natural History.

There are many other turtles and tortoises as interesting and colorful as these on the market. Most of these are apparently not in danger of extinction or of suffering a great reduction in numbers. If you must have something unusual, buy one of these species. The gophers, woods, spotted, and similar turtles have enough problems without being placed in a tank.

GIANT TORTOISES

The giant tortoises of the Pacific islands, especially the Galapagos, are a rather different story. Most of the Galapagos tortoises are, for all practical purposes, extinct. They are only "hanging on" because of their great longevity. Many of the specimens known to still exist, either in captivity or the wilds, are probably much too old to breed successfully. Even at best, the reproductive rate in giant tortoises is very low. Successful

The only place for giant tortoises is in the zoo—or rather in zoos having breeding colonies. Many of the races of giant tortoises will not successfully breed unless there are several pairs in a mating group. Photo by P. C. H. Pritchard.

breeding apparently often requires large numbers of tortoises together in one colony, so artificial cultivation can only be successful in zoos and parks which have colonies of the species. Individuals with one or two are merely watching their pet grow old. If you are ever offered a giant tortoise, and some pet shops do occasionally stock them, suggest that the dealer contact one of the established breeding colonies.

CHAPTER TEN.   HATCHING AND REARING

HATCHING

Not uncommonly, captive tortoises and turtles mate and lay fertile eggs.   If we provide a suitable place when furnishing the indoor or outdoor terrarium, the females will promptly lay their eggs there.   Aquatic turtles which have not been given a land part simply shed their eggs into the water.   Such eggs will never develop into small turtles, not even if they have been lying in the sun for several hours.

Once the eggs have been laid and the ground above them has been neatly levelled, the turtles forget about their eggs.   They leave the brooding to nature.   Now we must intervene, for the eggs require warmth to mature, and must be incubated.   There are many widely differing methods, but I would like to describe my own "hatchery", which I have tried out successfully many times, and in which numerous small turtles, lizards, and snakes have already hatched.

We need two aquaria, a fairly large one, half filled with water, and a smaller all-glass or plastic tank which is put inside the large tank.   Both aquaria are provided with cover strips which are inserted into the cover panes.   The cover strips of the small aquarium are flattened, i.e. not bevelled; those of the large aquarium, on the other hand, should be bevelled to prevent condensation water from collecting on them and dripping down on the small aquarium.   The water inside the large tank is kept at the desired temperature with an ordinary aquarium heater.

The small aquarium needs to be filled with peat. The peat is put into a bucket, and boiling water is poured over it. As soon as it has cooled, wring it out by hand or with a cloth. For our purposes, it is still too wet now and should be spread out on a plastic sheet and loosened up until it is as dry as needed. It has to feel just damp to the touch. The correct color is dark brown; if the peat is light brown, it is already too dry; if it is very dark, almost black, it is too wet. The peat thus prepared is put into the small aquarium to form a layer 15 centimeters thick. Put the eggs on top of it, taking care not to place them in contact with each other. The eggs are then lightly covered with a 5-centimeter thick layer of peat. During the entire period of maturation, too, the peat over the eggs has to be kept light and loose so that fresh air has access to the eggs all the time — otherwise the embryos would die of asphyxia.

If the peat is too damp, there is the same danger that the embryos will suffocate, for then the eggs get too little fresh air and easily grow moldy. Conversely, if the peat is too dry the eggs shrink owing to water depletion and small depressions form on the shell. We therefore have to check the moistness of the peat every day. If it is too dry, the cover glass of the small aquarium is opened slightly. If it is too damp, open the cover panes of both aquaria. In this way we can regulate the degree of moistness of the peat very well.

INCUBATION LENGTHS

The length of time required by the turtle eggs to mature varies greatly. The list below should give some idea of the time required. The temperature, in every case, lies within the range of 29 to 30° C.

Mediterranean spur-thighed tortoise *(Testudo graeca):* 78 to 81 days.
Hermann's tortoise *(Testudo h. hermanni):* 62 to 66 days.
Testudo h. robertmertensi: 69 to 71 days.

Margined tortoise *(Testudo marginata):* 68 to 71 days.
Leopard tortoise *(Geochelone pardalis):* 90 to 92 days.
European pond tortoise *(Emys orbicularis):* 68 to 71 days.
Spanish turtle *(Clemmys caspica leprosa)* 78 to 81 days.
Asiatic roofed turtle *(Kachuga tecta tecta):* 100 to 104 days.
North American cooters *(Pseudemys* species): 70 to 105 days.

If we discover a clutch of eggs in the terrarium, mark the top of the eggs with water color paint or nail polish. This is done so that when we move the eggs and put them into the incubator prepared for them, they come to lie in exactly the same position as before. They must not be turned, and the carrying, too, has to take place without any shaking or jarring.

CARE OF HATCHLINGS

Newly hatched aquatic turtles go into the water after just a few hours. Often they make for the water immediately after hatching, and there lie on the shallow shore for hours.

When do the young animals take food for the first time? This varies greatly. I have observed young animals feeding on the second day, and others which did not take food until the sixth, eighth, or even the ninth day. With newly hatched terrestrial turtles, too, it can happen that they do not accept any food until the fourth or fifth day. This is why newly hatched turtles must never be put into the terrarium with adult animals. They have to be kept separately in a small terrarium heated to 30° C.

Young aquatic turtles are offered large *Daphnia* or mosquito larvae as a first food; these are always popular. The first food of land turtles, on the other hand, consists of finely shredded lettuce and some fruit, particularly ripe bananas.

Good rearing results and quick weight gain can be achieved by giving a daily supplementary diet of chick rearing food and hardboiled eggs. One quarter of an egg is chopped finely and mixed with shredded lettuce or chives. The pressed chick food

Hatchling turtles possess a sharp tubercle, the egg tooth, on the nose. This tubercle allows them to cut their way out of the leathery egg shell.

(pellets) is highly nutritious. It contains calcium, mineral salts and vitamins, and in addition its main components consist of germinated wheat, alfalfa, oats, barley and corn. This food is also sold in powder form as fine grist; it is easy to mix with ripe bananas if we use a fork, and is eaten with relish by the little turtles — and the big ones, too, for that matter. Large turtles can be given the pressed food after it is moistened slightly. Never prepare more of this pressed food than the animals will eat within a short time.

A warm daily bath (32° C) with a very low water level is very good for the health of young turtles. It prevents constipation, which can occur frequently. Babies of the European land or water turtles are left in the heated terrarium all through the winter, since they could not survive hibernation in the cold cellar. To make sure the turtle babies eat and grow properly the whole winter, the temperature should never be lowered. By the following winter the animals are then strong enough to get through a shortened winter rest period of eight weeks unharmed.

CHAPTER ELEVEN.   HIBERNATION

All European land and water turtles and many North American ones, also, spend the cold season in a resting condition which is called hibernation or "winter sleep." Being animals of variable temperature, their body temperature drops in the same way as does the temperature of their surroundings. When October comes with its cool nights, the animals refuse all food and try to find a hiding place. Now they have to be removed from the outdoor enclosure and transferred to the hibernation box waiting for them. Animals which have been roaming freely inside the house or which were kept in the indoor terrarium are also prepared for hibernation at this time of the year. That is, the intestines of the animals have to be empty before hibernation begins; one week before transferring them to their winter box, therefore, stop giving them food.

We continue to heat the sleeping box and terrarium, as we have to bathe the turtles in lukewarm water several times during this week of fasting until they have ejected their feces. If bathing were to be carried out in the cold terrarium they would catch a chill. Afterwards we turn off the heat and, when the animals show a marked degree of rigidness, put them into the box.

The winter box has to be packed with a lot of filling material. The box must not be too small, because small boxes dry too quickly. Slits and cracks in the bottom of the box are sealed off with broad strips of plastic tape. Then the box is filled with a 15-centimeter deep layer of a 1:1 peat and sand mixture. The filling material should be moderately damp. On top of this we put the animals and cover them with a light layer of dry leaves. The box is wrapped in fine mesh netting to keep mice out.

Place the hibernating container in a room that is not heated but is safe from frost. A room in the basement is quite suitable provided it is not in the proximity of the central heating. If the room temperature were to be too high, the winter rigidity would not set in. The metabolism would not come to a standstill, and it is precisely this "standstill" that makes possible hibernation without feeding, often lasting for more than five months. Some weeks before this winter rest, as already mentioned, the turtles have to be given particularly nutritious food and plenty of it so that they are strong and well nourished when they go into hibernation.

As soon as the spring brings the first warm days, the turtles may leave the dark cellar. In a lukewarm bath they drink long draughts to replace the water they have lost. A few days later they take the first lettuce leaves. Now tadpoles and earthworms are the right food to give aquatic turtles back the fat deposits they have lost.

Aquatic turtles can also be hibernated in deep water basins with a thick layer of mud. But then the water basin has to be so deep that it never freezes to the bottom. European land tortoises, too, may be left in the outdoor enclosure if we have provided for them a deep pit filled with moss and dry leaves. But if the animals are left to hibernate here, there will usually be a few among them that die. Another thing that sometimes happens is that rats, mice, weasels, or skunks move into these warm quarters and then appease their hunger with the sleeping turtles.

A friend of mine, who is a very experienced turtle keeper, told me a that turtle found in the forest had been brought to him after escaping from his enclosure two years previously. He was able to identify the animal by the scar of a well-healed carapace injury. The astonishing thing about this observation is that this had taken place in a village high up in the Black Forest (580 meters above sea level), which means the animal had to endure two long, very severe winters in the Black Forest and, presumably buried in the soft forest ground, got through them unharmed.

CHAPTER TWELVE.

YOUR PET'S HEALTH

SALMONELLOSIS

Turtles are subject to as many diseases and illnesses as are warm-blooded animals such as cats and dogs. Unfortunately, however, very little is known about the prevention, cure, or even cause of most of their diseases. This chapter will briefly touch on some of the more common illnesses which can be treated. But first, it is necessary to say a few words about a subject of great importance to every keeper of turtles: SALMONELLA.

In the last few years this word has become the big bugaboo for dealers and keepers alike. There have been several incidences of severe illness connected to handling pet turtles, mostly red-ears, and a few have ended in death. Children are most commonly affected, probably because of their tendency to put pets near the mouth and not to wash hands after handling turtles. But before you give up on turtles, there are a few basic facts about salmonellosis which you should know.

Salmonellosis is a gastro-intestinal infection caused by bacteria belonging to the group *Salmonella*. There are well over 650 different strains of these bacteria, each varying slightly in their reaction to certain chemical and physical conditions. Twenty or more have been recorded from chickens and turkeys, about a dozen from hogs, and many from cats, dogs, cattle, horses, rodents, bone meal, fish meal, dried eggs, frozen foods, and many other sources. Many of these are relatively harmless, since large numbers of bacteria are necessary to produce any symptoms.

Although baby water turtles are carriers of *Salmonella* bacteria, care with cleanliness will reduce the chances of infection. Keep small children away from turtles! Photo by R. J. Church.

Salmonellosis has a 7 to 72 hour incubation period, followed by a sudden onset of diarrhea, vomiting, and abdominal pain. It is often necessary to hospitalize the patient, but usually the symptoms pass within a few days. Mortalities are very rare, as less than 3% of the cases result in death. Because of their small size, children require fewer bacteria to cause symptoms, and the disease is usually worse in children than adults.

Salmonellosis bacteria can be carried by many different methods. Contaminated water and food are the most likely sources, but many types of livestock feeds based on fish and bone meal have also been linked. Since heat destroys the bacteria, cooked food seldom has a large enough bacterial population to cause symptoms. Flies have also been incriminated in the mechanical spread of infections.

How do turtles fit in? Actually, only in a very minor way. Large-scale breeders often feed their turtles on scraps and offal from slaughter houses. Altough this is against the law in most states, it is a cheap way of obtaining food, so unscrupulous breeders simply evade the law. This offal often contains *Salmonella* bacteria, which are passed on to the young turtles. In addition, the turtles seem to have their own strain of the bacteria, which can build up large populations when the water is not changed frequently. In other words, *Salmonella* in turtles only becomes dangerous when the turtles are kept in unsanitary conditions.

In many, if not most, pet shops, young red-ears are kept in crowded containers and fed the wrong food. There are many weak and ill turtles in each batch, and these are often not removed. So the turtle you buy has a good chance of carrying a sizable population of *Salmonella* in its gut and on its body. This can easily be passed on to human hands by direct contact, or through contact with the water. If a child handles the turtle and then puts his hands near the mouth, or touches food eaten later, the infection will spread to man.

Prevention of the disease is comparatively easy. If there were a way of forcing breeders and pet shop owners to keep the turtles in the best, cleanest conditions, the disease would virtually disappear, at least in any way which would infect humans. Since this seems unlikely, the next best method is a period of quarantine and extreme cleanliness for the first few weeks after purchasing the turtle. Make sure that the water stays clean and excess food does not accumulate. Feed only good food, not possibly contaminated table scraps. Make sure that children (and adults) do not handle food after handling the turtles. These precautions should be no more trouble than washing your hands after going to the bathroom.

There has, unfortunately, been a move to outlaw the sale and keeping of pet turtles in many states, and perhaps eventually the entire country, because of their connection with salmonellosis. This seems ridiculous when you consider all the other possible sources of contamination.   In Sweden in 1953, there were 8,845 cases of salmonellosis, resulting in at least ninety deaths; the infection was traced to a packing house.   6,000 people came down with the disease in Germany; the outbreak was traced to contaminated Camembert cheese.*   Yet no one would suggest the outlawing of packing houses and Camembert cheese!   Just use sensible sanitary precautions, and you won't have anything to worry about.

It should be mentioned here that salmonellosis is not the same as botulism, as some people have tried to imply.   Botulism is a severe disease caused by an entirely different group of organisms.   It causes constipation and such side effects as double vision.   There is a 65% mortality rate.   Ptomaine poisoning, so famous for the upset stomachs after eating poorly prepared chicken sandwiches, is the same as salmonellosis.   Perhaps chicken sandwiches should be outlawed?

PNEUMONIA

Exposure to cold drafts can result in a condition known as either cold or pneumonia.   The first symptoms are a general uneasiness, loss of appetite, runny nose and eyes, and wheezy breathing.   If treated at this stage, the disease is usually cureable.   First make sure that all drafts are stopped, and the temperature is at least 75° F.   In winter, make sure the humidity is high; respiratory conditions like colds are made worse by low humidity.

Pneumonia usually responds to broad-spectrum antibiotics such as Acromycin and Aureomycin.   Use about 25 milligrams a day for three days (average 8 inch turtle).   Whenever you are using drugs, your veterinarian should be informed to direct your treatment; he will have to give you a prescription for the antibio-

* Hull, Thomas G. 1963.   Diseases Transmitted from Animals to Man.   Springfield, Ill.: Charles C. Thomas.   Chapter 6.

tics, anyway. Some people insist that antihistamines are also effective, and use commercial brands sold for human cold relief. Try about $\frac{1}{8}$ to $\frac{1}{4}$ tablet for a couple of days. Use a flat wooden probe or applicator to gently force the mouth open; the drugs may be dissolved in water and given in an eyedropper.

If the condition worsens and breathing becomes labored, the disease probably has the upper hand and your pet is dying. Probably nothing will help it once it reaches this point.

FUNGUS

Fungus usually takes the form of whitish growths on the limbs and shell or of a bright yellow growth on the jaws. Unless treated at once, the infection will spread and the turtle may die. Usually a bath in a mildly saline solution will clear it up. There are also many different types of fungicides available on the market, and most are good for turtles; this is especially true of the fish fungicides. Sulfathiazole ointments and baths are also good; a sulfathiazole bath is a good preventive, and should be given every week. Follow the directions on the label.

Unless the tank is also treated, the fungus will rapidly show up again. Clean the aquarium thoroughly and use a small amount of fish fungicide. It is a good idea to treat the turtle water every few weeks also.

CONSTIPATION AND DIARRHEA

Blockage of the gut is a serious illness which can occur in any turtle. Animals fed almost exclusively on packaged "turtle food" (dried flies) are especially likely to become constipated. This is also true of tortoises which have been on a monotonous diet. The best treatment is a soaking in a bath of luke-warm water. This helps elimination, and is good for the turtle anyway.

Sulfathiazole and other drugs are available in a wide variety of forms. Their use will prevent or cure many diseases of turtles. Photo courtesy of Wardley Pet Products.

Diarrhea is also common in tortoises, and can be caused by the food or temperature. Make sure there are no drafts and that the cage temperature is high enough. Change the diet for a few days and see if there is any change. Make sure the turtle is getting enough vitamins and that the diet has not grown too monotonous. Starchy foods will also help control the condition, but they are not always good for the tortoise.

SOFT SHELL

This is the most common and deadliest of the deficiency diseases of turtles. It results from a lack of sufficient calcium in the diet and kills thousands of young turtles each year. The easiest cure is to prevent it. Equip each tank with a source of calcium, such as the plaster turtles or shells sold in pet shops.   This partially dissolves in the water and helps a little.   Bathe the turtles regularly, especially juveniles, in one of the commercial turtle baths which contains calcium salts and sulfathiazole.   Add calcium salts or bone meal to your turtles' food every few days, and try to make sure that he eats it; if it just falls to the bottom of the tank it won't do much good.   Give vitamin supplements at least once a week, because a turtle in good overall health is much less prone to succumb to calcium deficiency (or any other illness, for that matter).

If your turtle is already soft when purchased, give it calcium supplements in every form you can think of.   Put them in the water, the food, and even in the drinking water.   Bathe regularly and often.   If the turtle is otherwise healthy, it will usually recover.

Remember that a large amount of calcium is needed by young, actively growing turtles.   It is much better to give an excess than too little.

SORE EYES

First, never buy a turtle with "pop eye" if you have any choice. This condition is very common in shipments of young red-ears, and is often fatal.   Eye inflammations which develop after purchase are probably due to dirty water and bacterial infection. Eye ointments are available for turtles, usually containing some type of antibiotic.   If this is not available, resort again to the old reliable turtle bath and sulfathiazole — it will help.   Clean the tank completely, and add new water.   Make sure the diet is well balanced.   Recovery is usually rapid.

Ointments are also good for use on rubbed areas of the carapace and plastron, perhaps caused by rough basking rocks or bottom gravel.   Make sure the water and bottom are clean, or fungus is likely to get a foothold.   Replace the rough material with smoother gravel, sand, or wood.   Never use concrete if anything else is available.   Turtles and tortoises often develop sores on the

Heavy erosion on the plastron of this *Siebenrockiella crassicollis* was caused by a concrete floor. Photo by M. F. Roberts.

The brown spots at the bases of the legs in this *Hompus areolatus* are ticks. External parasites are quite common in newly imported animals, but they may be killed by covering them with a layer of Vaseline or heavy mineral oil. Photo by M. F. Roberts.

limbs from rough bottom material, so be selective in your choice of tank furnishings.

GENERAL CARE

The best way to take care of your turtle's health is to prevent the situations which lead to disease. First, make sure the temperature is always high enough for the species you are keeping; in the winter, make sure the humidity is not too low for your tortoise. Second, make sure the surroundings are always clean and sanitary; no old food, litter, drinking water, or feces should be allowed to accumulate. Third, make sure the diet is well balanced and complete; use vitamin and calcium supplements freely; make sure the diet does not get monotonous, and that the food is always clean and fresh. Fourth, always pay attention to your turtle's general well-being; observe it often for symptoms of fungus, sore eyes, constipation; make sure that it is actually eating what you are feeding it, and not just mixing it into the bottom of the tank.

If this were a dog or cat book, I would close by advising you to become familiar with a good local veterinarian and use his services often. However, there are few vets today who are familiar with the ills of turtles. There are general conditions, such as pneumonia and bacterial infections, in which the treatment is similar for all groups of animals. In these cases, the veterinarian's help is vital. Turtles are growing in popularity, and more people are keeping turtles as pets, not just playthings. Hopefully some day the knowledge and drugs necessary to treat turtle diseases will be more complete and widespread.

INDEX

Page numbers in **bold** type indicate an illustration.

Spanish turtle, **81**
Spiny soft-shell turtle, **99-100**
Spotted turtle, **64**, 106, **108**
Spurred tortoise, **38**
Sternotherus odoratus, **53**
Stinkpot, **53**

T

Terrapene carolina, **46-47**, **50-51**
Terrapene carolina bauri, **37**, **47**,
   50
Terrapene carolina major, 50
Terrapene carolina triunguis, 50
Terrapene ornata, 37, 50
Terrapin, **9**
Terrarium, 12-23
Testudo graeca, **31-32**, **33-34**
Testudo graeca zarudnyi, **33**
Testudo hermanni, 30-31, 34, 35
Testudo hermanni robertmerten-
   si, 30
Testudo horsfieldi, **32**
Testudo marginata, **34**, 35

Three-lined box turtle, **52**, 92
Ticks, 24, 124
Trionyx ferox, **57**, 100
Trionyx muticus, 100
Trionyx spiniferus, **99**-100
Tubifex worms, 74

U

Ultraviolet light, 28, 72

V

Vitamins, 27-28

W

Western box turtle, 37, 50
Wood turtle, 106-**107**
Wood turtles, 106-108

Y

Yellow-bellied turtle, 83, 85
Yellow-legged tortoise, **36**, 43
Yellow-spotted Amazon turtle
   11, **95-96**